bestofbritish
CLASSIC CARS

Jon Stroud

bestofbritish
CLASSIC CARS

First published in the UK in 2015

© Demand Media Limited 2015

www.demand-media.co.uk

Printed and bound in Europe

ISBN 978-1-910540-68-8

Contents

MG

04 - 13	First of a New Line – the MGA
14 - 15	Return of the Midget
20 - 29	MGB – An Icon
30 - 33	End of an Era

ASTON MARTIN

34 - 35	International
36 - 37	Le Mans
38 - 39	Mark II and Ulster
40 - 41	15/98
42 - 43	Atom
44 - 45	2-Litre Sports ('DB1')
46 - 47	DB2
48 - 49	DB Mark III
50 - 51	DB4
52 - 53	DB4 GT
54 - 55	DB5
56 - 57	DB6
58 - 59	DBS and DBS V8
60 - 61	Lagonda
62 - 63	V8 Vantage
64 - 65	V8 Volante
66 - 67	Bulldog
68 - 69	V8 Zagato
70 - 71	Virage
72 - 73	Vantage
74 - 75	DB7
76 - 77	DB7 Vantage
78 - 79	Vanquish
80 - 81	DB7 Zagato
82 - 83	DB American Roadster 1
84 - 85	DB7 GT
86 - 87	DB9
88 - 89	Vanquish S
90 - 91	V8 Vantage
92 - 93	Rapide Concept
94 - 95	DBS
96 - 99	James Bond and Aston Martin

E-TYPE JAGUAR

100 - 115	Series 1
116 - 119	Series 2
120 - 127	Series 3

MG

First of a New Line – the MGA

FOR THE ABINGDON WORKFORCE the prospect of working on an all-new modern sports car was a cause of great excitement. At last here was a chance to give the world the MG car they had deserved for so long. There was only one place the designers needed to look for inspiration – the record breaking EX175. The intention was to take the car from the drawing board to full scale production within a 12-month window.

Roy Brocklehurst's original prototype chassis needed little modification to become suitable for the road and the TF developed independent front suspension and rack and pinion steering were more than capable for the new car. The Midget's adapted XPEG motor was,

however, deemed inappropriate having already been pushed to its physical and performance limits. Instead, the durable 1489cc BMC B-series four-cylinder OHV already fitted to the ZA Magnette was to be used, as was the saloon's four-speed gearbox. Although hardly the most inspiring of engines in standard form the MG technicians were able to weave their magic and add some sparkle with the addition of a second carburettor and an increase in compression. The result was a hike in power from 50bhp to a more impressive 68bhp – an increase of 36%!

A plan was hatched to launch the TF replacement to the public early in June 1955 and then to immediately take three

of the machines to the Le Mans 24 Hour – a brave test of any car let alone an untested one fresh off the production line – and Abingdon may well have achieved the near impossible in turning the car around within a year had it not been for production problems beyond their control. The new sleek, stream-lined Enever bodywork was being man-ufactured by Swindon based Pressed Steel who were, at the time, experiment-ing with new production techniques including the use of plastic dies to shape the metal body panels. For all of their efforts this technology proved infeasible and only served to hinder manufactur.

Rather than show an unfinished pro-duction car the three Le Mans racers were quickly finished and revealed as the new EX182 racing prototypes. This decision may, in the long run, have acted in MG's favour; softening the blow for the MG traditionalists for whom the marque stood for squared-off bonnets, long running boards and that upright radiator grille. Under the

admirably on the Le Mans tarmac, causing quite a stir on their arrival at the paddock, resplendent in British Racing Green with polished wire wheels, low screen and additional radiator-mounted spot lamp. However, the race itself had a far less glorious outcome when, after two hours of racing, a works Mercedes-Benz 300SLR driven by Frenchman Pierre Levegh crashed after clipping the Austin-Healey of Lance Macklin which in turn was braking heavily to avoid the Jaguar of Mike Hawthorn. Levegh's car was launched into the air before ricocheting off a bank and into the densely packed spectators. At about the same time one of the EX182s also crashed at White House before catching fire and seriously injuring its driver Dick Jacobs. Despite the accident, officials decided to allow the race to continue ostensibly to prevent any further panic and to keep the access roads clear for emergency vehicles. Only when reports confirmed the death toll to be in excess of 80 people did the leading Mercedes-Benz team withdraw as a mark of respect. The two remaining MGs were among the 21 cars that finished from 60 starters, achieving 86.17mph and 81.97mph averages.

At last the production MG was finally

guise of being the Le Mans MG racer it was easy to introduce the sleek radical shape with the minimum fuss and maximum exposure.

Whilst never in serious overall contention, the three MGs performed

launched to the public in September 1955 before being taken to the premiere motor shows in Paris, Frankfurt and London. The name Midget had been dropped in favour of a new designation and so the MGA was born. In a perfectly staged test, five production cars were pitted against a Le Mans racer in a one hour test on the Montlhéry track: the EX182 recording an average speed of 112.36mph with its road-going cousin covering a remarkable 102.54mph. Even the usually sceptical motoring press were full of praise; Autocar and Autosport both making top speeds approaching 100mph with acceleration to 60mph of around 15 seconds, some 20% quicker than the TF. Autosport commented that "if you want one, hurry up and get in the queue" and even their more conservative rival, Motor, agreed that the MGA "must be summed up as enthusiastically as it was everywhere received". This was more than enough to convince the public that MG were back on track and once again making true sports cars.

The MGA was a resounding and immediate success. At just £595 it comfortably undercut the opposition for price (its BMC stablemate, the Austin-Healey 100 cost £155 more before tax) whilst offering equal, if not superior, performance and driveability. Over its first year of production 13,410 cars were produced, over 3,000 more than were constructed during the entire four-year lifespan of the much lauded TC Midget. Of these, nearly 10,600 machines were exported to the up-and-coming United States market. Combined with sales of the Magnette, Abingdon was now producing well over 20,000 cars per year.

By this time, the ZA Magnette had been modified and renamed the ZB.

Externally the reworked saloon was instantly identifiable by a tapered chrome side strip on the front wing and doors. More significant changes were hidden away under the curved bonnet. Larger carburettors fed an enhanced B-series engine with an improved cylinder head and raised compression to generate 68bhp – a 13% increase in power – which, when allied to a higher final drive ratio improved top speed and acceleration. Also available to ZB owners as an option was the ill-fated Manumatic transmission – a primitive version of the modern Tiptronic gear-

BELOW The MGA with its beautiful streamlined body

change found on many luxury cars. Using a complex system of vacuums, servos and hydraulics it offered the driver the ability to change gear without the need for a clutch. However, its fragile and over-complicated construction led to many reliability problems for the few motorists brave enough to specify its inclusion, and it was soon abating.

1957 and there was no sign of interest in the MGA dropping off; in fact, quite the opposite was happening. Production increased to an amazing 20,571 cars with an unbelievable 17,195 of the sportster finding their way across the Atlantic. The nation so used to the heavyweight Detroit steel had taken the little MG to its heart.

With increasing speeds becoming available to everyday motorists it became apparent that the rag-topped roof convertible cars were starting to reveal their shortcomings with drafts, leaks and wind-noise being all too com-

ABOVE The MGA represented very good value for money in the mid Fifties

mon. In addition to working on a new hood design, MG decided to first offer a detachable hard top roof before launching a fully closed in coupé. An altogether quieter and more civilised car, the new slippery shape gave an instant increase in performance with speeds in excess of 100mph being easily attainable.

If records were being broken in sales and export, it was nothing compared to what was being achieved by the competitions department. EX179 had made another successful appearance stateside taking 16 international records during August 1956 including a flying 10 miles at 170.15 and a marathon 12-hour run at 141.71. The car returned again in 1957 and, powered by a smaller 948cc OHV based on the type used in the sedentary Morris Minor, recorded a 118mph average for the 12-hour run whilst returning an enormous 49.8mpg. The icing on the cake for the MG team was a 143.47mph flying mile with driving ace Phil Hill at the wheel.

Aware that EX179 was nearing the peak of its development potential, Syd Enever had once again put pen to paper and designed what he believed would be the next generation of MG record breakers. With a tubular chassis and mid-mounted engine the driver was positioned much further forward than in previous EX cars. In fact, so far forward that his toes would all but graze the inside of the elliptical nose cone of the amazing lightweight aluminium teardrop body – a form so aerodynamic that it created 30% less drag than EX179 and sat with the line of its bodywork a mere 76cm from the ground with the top of the cockpit just 20cm higher still. To power it a modified twin-cam 1489cc B-series engine was fitted with a Shorrock supercharger, an immensely powerful unit designed for use in commercial vehicles. Stopping power was provided by a single rear-mounted brake which, when activated, was cooled by air channelled via a small bodywork flap mechanically linked to the brake pedal. The result was a super-slippery record car with almost 300bhp on tap with the stopping power of an ocean liner!

Enever and his MG colleagues had two clear targets in mind for EX181 as this new car was christened. The first was to

BELOW This MG displays the soft top version with its high roof and large windscreen

break the class F record for 1500cc cars that had been set by Goldie Gardner back in 1939 and, as yet, stood un-bettered. The second objective was to push the record further, much further — and to achieve four miles per minute! To their mind there was just one man suitable for the job: Grand Prix hero Stirling Moss.

After a number of delays, 27-year-old Moss started his record attempt on the afternoon of 23 August 1957. With speed calculated using the average of two runs in opposite directions the records fell one by one; first the flying kilometre at 245.64mph, then the mile at 245.11mph and next the five kilometre and five mile at 243.08mph and 235.69mph respec-

tively. Finally the 10 kilometre was taken at an astounding 224.70mph. In all, five international records had been bettered by at least 20% - a remarkable achievement in a sport where improvements are usually measured in hundredths of a second.

A further boost in MGA performance came in 1958. Finding themselves well in favour with their BMC masters, MG decided to create a high-performance version of the phenomenally popular MGA with a view to once again enticing the amateur racers who had provided the marque with so much pre-war publicity.

The beating heart of this special, the brainchild of the ZA Magnette designer

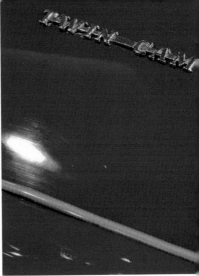

ABOVE 1958-1960
MGA Twincam Roadster

Gerald Palmer, was a 1588cc DOHC developed from the same 1489cc OHV utilised in the existing MGA. By using this same cylinder block it negated any need to change the chassis or gearbox arrangement – the modified twin-cam unit with its cross-flow head and huge 1¾" SU carburettors instead dropping neatly into place. Dunlop supplied both the braking system and the wheels; the standard drums being abandoned in favour of an all-disc system and the wire wheels being replaced by race inspired centre-locking steel ones with light-alloy centres to save further weight. Other than the different wheels, the only distinguishing marks of this per-

formance model were "Twin Cam" badges located neatly on the boot lid and adjacent to the bonnet vents.

The MGA Twin Cam went as fast as it looked with a top speed of around 114mph and acceleration to 60mph in a shade over nine seconds. With handling undeniably improved, MG should have been on to an instant winner. Its £854 10s price tag, although £180 more than a standard MGA was still considerably less than other less exotic marques of the day and once again the motoring press rained praise over Abingdon's latest achievement. But the car soon gained an unwelcome reputation for unreliability with holed pistons being a

MGA production continued to go from strength to strength. On the back of the Twin Cam project the standard A was uprated to a 1588cc OHV known as the MGA 1600. The increase in capacity generated an additional 7.5bhp. Little else changed with the model save for some minor cosmetic differences such as redesigned lights and optional coloured fabric hoods. A Mark II update was to come in June 1961. With the reshaped cylinder head bored out to 1622cc and the use of modified pistons, con-rods and crankshaft, the engine was stronger than ever producing over 90bhp – an increase of 10.5bhp over the MGA1600 MKI – making the last of the pushrod MGAs as fast and capable a motor as the doomed Twin Cam but without the problems of reliability.

MG had at last lain to rest the ghosts of its past; the MGA having sold an incredible 101,081 cars in its seven-year life. However, the marque was about to turn over another chapter in its history and one that would see the creation of the most iconic MG of all time.

LEFT The MGA Twin Cam's distinctive bonnet vents

familiar problem due to pre-ignition caused by the use of low octane fuel. Despite constant modification by the factory it was not enough to reinstall public confidence. Less than 2000 MGAs were produced before the model was retired late in 1959.

To the disappointment of the Abingdon staff the ZB Magnette was discontinued in 1958. It was replaced by the uninspired Magnette Mark III which, to the indignation of the MG staff, was nothing more than a re-badged 1½ litre Wolseley and was the first of the marque to be constructed outside of Abingdon since the company had moved there way back in 1930.

Return of the Midget

AT THE TURN OF THE 1960s MG dealers were forced once again to look on with envious green eyes at the Austin-Healey showrooms just as they had done eight years before with the launch of the Healey 100. They were all too aware how Leonard Lord's lack of commitment to the company had forced them to produce an inferior model, the TF Midget, long past its sell by date and threatening the company's very existence. Only with the production of the MGA had the balance been redressed. But now Austin-Healey had something new in their arsenal that served to fill a bright new gap in the market and what's more it was being constructed in MG's own Abingdon workshops.

In its first full year of production the Austin-Healey Sprite, as this new sportster was called, had sold over 21,000 units. The design brief had been simple from the outset – to produce a compact, cheap sports car capable of recapturing the adventurous young spirit that, in pre-war years, had made cars like the M-type Midget so popular. Based on the 42.5bhp 948cc BMC A-type engine, gearbox and front suspension of the little Austin A35 saloon and combined with the pinpoint rack-and-pinion steering of the Morris Minor, the Sprite was the first BMC sports car to be constructed around a monocoque body whereby the chassis and body panels were built as a single unit – rigidity being created by integral box-section members and the transmission tunnel. The resulting package, which had quickly become nicknamed the Frogeye Sprite due to its protruding "pod" headlamps which gave the car the appearance

ABOVE A race-prepared Sprite driven at speed in the Scottish Highlands

of an amphibian, albeit a very fast one, was light, fairly quick and immensely fun to drive. However, it was not without fault. In some respects the body shell was too rigid for the size of car – on an uneven surface high-speed cornering could be described as a series of hops, skips and jumps – and remarkably the body itself was without external access to the boot. (Perhaps in these modern days of car crime this is a design feature that should be revisited?)

Word soon got around of the problems and with the vociferous motoring press capable of praising and damning in equal measure, these criticisms caused a drop in sales during the model's second year. The solution in the eyes of BMC was to build a Mark II Sprite which would serve to address these faults whilst giving an opportunity to improve power and handling.

The man chosen to lead the project was none other than MG's own Syd Enever. The creation of a redesigned car created another opportunity for BMC – to use this new model as a platform to create a comparable MG.

This was to be far more than a quick wash and brush up for the Sprite. The same original body shell was used but to this were added redesigned wings (without the bulging-eye headlamps) and a totally new bonnet that cleverly made use of all the original mountings. The curved rear of the car was cut away and a new rear deck welded into place and boot lid fitted. Furthermore, to improve interior space a large section of the rear panel was cut away behind the seats. Even the BMC A-Series motor underwent substantial changes. Larger inlet valves, 1¼" SU carburettors, a revised crankshaft design and raised compression all helped provide an additional 4bhp.

The car was launched to the public in 1961 as both the Austin-Healey Sprite MkII and as the MG Midget MkI – known affectionately by the Abingdon engineers as the Spridget. Although at £669 15s 10d the Midget was just over £38 more expensive, MG owners benefited from a slightly higher overall specification enjoying the delights of an improved interior, double sliding side window flaps and, of course, the inimitable MG badge and grille.

After combined sales in excess of 36,500 cars, a year later a revised MkI Midget / MkII Sprite was launched to the public. Having had its engine capacity increased to 1098cc and now producing a healthy 55bhp, and the fitment of an improved clutch and synchromesh and front Lockheed disk brakes, the new model, although not designated as a new mark, was much improved in every respect not least performance and handling with a top speed now approaching 90mph.

Late 1962 saw the arrival of two new models in the MG range: the MGB Roadster – brought in to replace the now ageing MGA – and the MG1100 Saloon which, in many respects, was often overlooked, thanks to the success

of its sportier stablemates, despite its revolutionary design.

Over its lifetime the 1100 was produced in many forms thanks to the "badge-engineering" that was prevalent within the BMC organisation, bearing the motifs of Morris, Wolseley, Austin, Riley and Vanden Plas in addition to MG. Designed under the watchful eye of Austin Mini creator Alec Issigonis, and styled by Pininfarina, the Italian body stylists responsible for iconic cars as

diverse as the Peugeot 404 and the Ferrari Enzo, the saloon was a symbol of automotive modernity. In its MG guise it was powered by the indomitable BMC A-Series 1098cc four-cylinder motor but, for the first time, it was transversally mounted with twin carburettors and drove the front wheels. The ground-breaking Hydrolastic suspension system, a creation of Alex Moulton, was the first of its kind to utilise linked hydraulics. Referred to as being "suspensational" in

RIGHT MG1100 was
introduced into the
American market as an
upscale and larger
version of the Mini

the MG promotional film Magic Carpet
(notably, with Graham Hill at the wheel)
the system allowed the car to remain far
more stable in cornering by reducing
pitch and roll.

Later in its life the MG1100 with a
redesigned body shell benefited from a
new version of the BMC A-Series – a
1275cc single carburettor variant
designed for the Mini Cooper S albeit in
a lower state of tune. For some time the
MG1100 and the MG1300 were sold
side by side until, in 1968, the smaller-
engined model was discontinued at
which time the larger machine gained a
second carburettor and an increase in
power of 7bhp. A final revision of the
MG1300 took place in 1968 with the
introduction of the MkII – a generally
updated two-door model with a mod-
ernised interior and a more potent
70bhp engine that remained in the
range until being dropped in 1972.

During this time the Midget had also
undergone a series of changes and modifications. 1962 saw the arrival of an all
new machine, the Triumph Spitfire 4,
launched to compete directly with the
Midget and Sprite in the blossoming
small sports car market. Powered by a
1147cc straight-four this Michelotti-

designed roadster instantly put pressure
on the BMC motors, being quicker and
better appointed with modern luxuries
such as winding windows and a more
luxurious cockpit.

BMC's response was the MkII
Midget /MkIII Sprite. Strengthened
with an uprated crankshaft and
MG1100 cylinder head, the 1098cc A-
series engine's power was increased
4bhp to 59bhp. Now capable of around
92mph it was at least back on par with

relocation of the door lock and handle which had to be completely relocated to allow enough room for the glass to fall into the door. Fortunately these efforts appeared worth their trouble and the following year sales increased to over 22,000 cars.

Just as the 1275cc Mini Cooper S engine had benefited the MG Saloon so, in 1966, it was to benefit the Midget and Sprite as the MkIII / MkIV variants were introduced. Once again the motor was fitted in a lower state of tune as a means of maintaining affordability but, nevertheless, it still managed to produce a respectable 65bhp with improvements in both acceleration and top speed. Other modifications included a larger, more powerful clutch, dual servo brakes and a completely redesigned folding hood. Once again it seemed as if the Spridget was back on a par with its Triumph rival but, as always seemed to be the case with the Abingdon marque, it was all change in the boardroom and soon MG would be presented with a whole new set of trials and tribulations.

the Triumph in terms of top speed. Amusingly, upgrading the engine was probably the easiest task that presented itself to the Abingdon engineers – creating wind-up windows was another matter altogether! First the doors themselves had to be thickened to allow enough room for the winder mechanism and the glass. This encroached on the cabin space to such an extent that the door-mounted map pockets had to be discarded. More significant was the

MGB – An Icon

FOR ONCE IN THEIR EXISTENCE, the MG factory found themselves with the almost unheard of luxury of time when it came to developing the successor to the amazingly successful MGA. No sooner had the marque's premier sports car hit the streets than Syd Enever and his Abingdon design team set to creating what was destined to become the greatest MG of all time. Whilst automotive technology was moving along at a pace, other aspects of the motor industry never seemed to change. As always, the BMC purse strings were pulled tight shut with the excuse being that MG were not seen as profitable compared to other motor manufacturers within the corporation due to some archaic and thoroughly biased accounting methods used within the group.

Enever's first instinct was to base the car on the running gear of the MGA so in 1957 specialist Pietro Frua, the Turin based designer responsible for the graceful and exotic lines of many a Maserati, was sent a 1500 chassis. However, the resulting designs, although stunning to look at, were considered impractical to

ABOVE 1964 MGB works rally replica

build and unsuitable for the relatively small engine size of the British sportster. A new approach was sought closer to home through the minds of general manager John Thornley and Don Hayter, both of whom had spent a considerable amount of time in the employ of Aston Martin and were familiar with the development of the DB2.

A decision was taken to develop a monocoque – this was increasingly becoming the norm in sports car design and had just been implemented in the BMC-designed Austin-Healey Sprite and its MG Midget twin. Hayter had already penned an open-topped roadster body styling based on EX181 with the MGA chassis in mind but it was not a difficult task to rework the drawings into a practicable form for an integrated monocoque design. Soon the Abingdon technicians set to work on creating a mock-up which, when viewed by the BMC management, was given immediate prototype approval.

All through this process the Cowley bean-counters were keeping a close eye on the project and Thornley was aware that additional funds over the production budget would in no way be forthcoming. Here lay the problem. The original plan to build the MGA's successor had been based around the desire to utilise the existing chassis, or at least a variant of it. However, as there was little point designing an outdated machine, things had changed and now a unitary construction was on the cards and with it a bill for substantially increased tooling costs. Unbeaten by the prospect Thornley approached the bodywork manufacturers Pressed Steel who had recently moved from their Cowley base to the new town of Swindon enticed by government incentives promoting the expanding Wiltshire location. Keen to capture MG's business, a deal was struck whereby a large proportion of the set up and tooling charges were to be included in the cost of each body produced rather than as an upfront charge. Without this agreement it is unlikely the car would ever have been built.

With the new agreement in place development quickly progressed. The monocoque soon took form; to the front was a box section consisting of the inner wings, front panel and engine compartment, in the middle a second box comprising of the front floor, bulkhead and scuttle and to the back the boot, rear inner wings and the rear panels. Further box sections stiffened the floor and formed mountings for the outer bodywork and suspension. Initial experiments with a rear coil-spring arrangement were abandoned in favour of the ubiquitous (and substantially cheaper) half-elliptical system that had graced MGs for many years. If it ain't broke don't fix it!

A major decision for the Abingdon team was to be their choice of engine. It had been assumed that the obvious candidate for inclusion was the 1588cc unit of the MGA Twin-Cam but this idea was soon shelved when it became apparent that the motor was forever plagued with reliability issues. A second proposal was to modify the 2639cc six-cylinder C-Series engine used in the Austin A90 Westminster by removing two cylinders to produce a 1760cc four-

ABOVE An MGB GT car at the 1965 London Motor Show

cylinder. After considerable deliberation a choice was made and once more it was the MGA's trustworthy 1622cc B-Series that was chosen to star. This itself soon proved to be somewhat lacking in power but, by good fortune alone, it was discovered that there were already plans afoot within BMC to enlarge its capacity to 1798cc in preparation for a new saloon car. For once fate had smiled upon MG, saving them from further substantial and unexpected development costs.

The launch of the all new MGB took place at the 1962 London Motor Show to great acclaim. The press had a field day with superlatives. "Superior" remarked Autocar, "delightful" said The Motor, "the best all-round sports-car on the market" extolled Motoring News. And so it went on. The press and public alike recognised that the Abingdon factory had pulled off something rather special and had created an instant

ABOVE An MGB GT car at the 1965 London Motor Show

ABOVE New MGB
exhibited at the
International Auto Show

classic; a true icon of British motoring.

All noted how spacious the new car was, not only compared to its predecessor but to pretty much all of the existing competition. Amazingly this had been achieved in a car some five inches shorter than the MGA. MG had realised that not only were they growing up, so were their customers. Expectations were now far higher than they had been in the past. Gone were the days of rough and ready sports cars. The public no longer had a taste for sitting in a cramped cockpit, being battered by the elements and being aurally assaulted by noisy engines. They wanted the sporting image but with the luxuries afforded to the owners of upmarket saloon cars. So sliding side

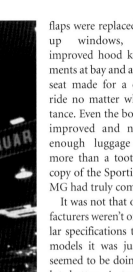

flaps were replaced with wind up windows, a vastly improved hood kept the elements at bay and an adjustable seat made for a comfortable ride no matter what the distance. Even the boot had been improved and now offered enough luggage space for more than a toothbrush and copy of the Sporting Life. The MG had truly come of age.

It was not that other manufacturers weren't offering similar specifications to their new models it was just that MG seemed to be doing it a whole lot better. A top speed of around 108mph and acceleration to 60 in 12.1 seconds set it on a par with the others in terms of outright performance. However, this machine wasn't trying to be a race car for the road. Its handling was quick and precise but nevertheless civilised making the B a far more driveable motor than many of its supposed rivals and at £690 it was considerably cheaper with the Triumph TR4 £60 dearer and the Austin-Healey 3000 costing a whopping £895.

The positivity of the press and public was easily converted into sales and by the end of 1963 almost 28,000 cars had been produced of which almost 80% were exported (in most cases to the United States). The following year sales of the MGB increased to 26,542 units whilst Abingdon's total production, including Austin-Healey output, exceeded 55,000 cars for the first time.

As sales boomed across the MG range it was time to deal yet another ace from the pack. Announced in October 1965, this came in the form of the super-sleek MGB GT coupé. If the MGB roadster had been regarded as a good car then this machine was truly amazing.

Priced at £825 it still measured favourably against its obvious rivals but now had the looks that comfortably put the opposition in the shade. Thornley later claimed that this was a car "in which no managing director would be ashamed to turn up at the office" – probably a statement that would ring true to this day. At last drivers were fully protected from the elements and treated to a quieter and more refined driving environment! The beautiful transformation of the original MGB to a stunning fastback had been undertaken by

Battista Pininfarina, the designer who already had the iconic Ferrari 275 and Lancia Flaminia in his portfolio and whose company would go on to create the Ferrari Enzo and P4/5 in the twenty-first century. Although considerably heavier having gained 100kgs in roof and reinforcement, the GT performed superbly with acceleration barely affected and top speed actually increased, thanks to the more aerodynamic profile of the closed styling. The handling also improved considerably as the stiffer body negated any degree of body flex that had been encountered in the standard MGB.

Revisions were made to both models towards the end of 1967 with the fitment of a new, fully synchromeshed gearbox, an alternator to replace the ageing dynamo and a different radiator. For the first time, automatic transmission was offered as an optional extra. Cosmetic changes, however, were minimal and mostly centred around the cockpit and with US safety legislation very much in mind.

For the London Motor Show of that year another model was launched. The new MGC, at first glance, appeared just the same as an MGB or GT but closer

inspection revealed a number of interesting alterations and additions to the original design. For a start, bigger wheels and tyres were tucked away under the arches making the car stand a little taller whilst the bonnet now sporting a large bulge across its centre gave subtle clues to what lay beneath.

The engine for the MGC had, unusually, been developed from scratch for the project following a series of attempts to create a large capacity sports car which, like the Spridget, could be sold in both Healey and MG guises to replace the ageing Austin-Healey 3000. The original project had faltered after Healey, unhappy with yet another close association with MG, elected to pull out (a decision that would be their undoing when the big-cc Healey was soon discontinued) but engine development had continued with the MGB body shell in mind. Well, partially in mind. Far from fitting like a glass slipper the resulting 2912cc six-cylinder motor

had to be positively shoehorned into position after huge modifications to the engine bay and transmission.

With 150bhp on tap this was the most powerful production MG to date. Public expectation was high – all those horses harnessed to the sublime MGB would surely create an impressive car packed with speed and muscle? Well, the speed was there with 124mph being comfortably attainable but muscular it was not. The engine just didn't produce enough low-end torque to match the handling potential of the body and suspension. Whilst far from being a failure of design it simply lacked the sparkle that the press, public and most probably MG themselves had anticipated. Priced at £1101 16s 10d for the standard model and £1249 6s 6d for the GT it failed to capture the imagination and was discontinued after just two years and a

BELOW 1968 MGC GT

total of 9002 cars produced.

An altogether more impressive big-cc MGB was launched a few years later in 1973. Designated the MGB GT V8, it had benefited from yet another BMC group corporate merger and the formation of the British Leyland Motor Corporation in 1968 and the engineering exploits of former Mini racer Ken Costello.

Costello had been modifying standard customer MGB cars by removing the trusty 1798cc B-Series motor and fitting a British built version of the 3.5 litre Buick V8 used in the new Range Rover that was mated to the original gearbox and axle via a larger clutch. The resulting car was by all accounts pretty outstanding with a top speed approaching 130mph and acceleration to 60 in less than eight seconds. Crucially, the big V8 produced a massive amount of torque, about 80% more than the 1.8 litre four-

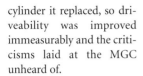

cylinder it replaced, so driveability was improved immeasurably and the criticisms laid at the MGC unheard of.

Aware of the success of the Costello-built cars the British Leyland board sanctioned the development of a prototype V8-powered machine of their own. This was partly a reaction to the recent release of Ford's new transatlantic-inspired Capri which, from the outset had been offered in variants of up to 3.0 litres. The Abingdon machine once again used the Range Rover V8, although this time it was coupled to a heavily modified clutch and gearbox. Larger disks and callipers were fitted to the front braking system whilst the suspension system was upgraded by the use of stiffer racing springs. To help keep everything in a straight line wider wheels and tyres were specified.

On its release there was no doubting that the MGB V8 was an impressive car and gone were the criticisms of the gutless MGC's poor low speed capabilities.

There were, however, a couple of new issues that soon raised their heads. The first related to the actual design of the car. There was nothing wrong with the MGB shape of course but there was nothing physically about the V8 that separated it from the rest of the range save for the V8 moniker fastened to the radiator grille. The exterior appeared the same, as did the interior. For a car priced at almost £2300, about £600 more than the standard MGB, this was a severe oversight. The reality was simple; MG themselves would have included all the bells and whistles in the factory store given half the chance but it was the Leyland board with their tunnel vision who, as always, held the purse strings.

The second problem was way out of the hands of MG or British Leyland. Syria and Egypt had attacked Israel and instigated the Yom Kippur War which, although a short-lived conflict, caused massive worldwide oil shortages. Pump prices rose dramatically and, between 1973 and 1975, the cost in the UK of a gallon of petrol leapt from 38.7 to 73.2 pence – more than enough to discourage many from the purchase of a large capacity sports car. In total only 2591 MGB V8s were manufactured.

End of an Era

THE 1970S WERE A TIME OF CHANGE for the MGB, MG itself and the lumbering behemoth that was British Leyland. International legislation, boardroom indifference and questionable loyalties all had a part to play in the fortunes and misfortunes of the proud Abingdon marque. Both the MGB and the Midget found themselves subjected to countless forced modifications and changes although few of these alterations could honestly be described as improvements.

The first real problems were encountered in 1971 when at the behest of the National Highways Traffic Safety Administration (NHTSA), the US government body essentially employed to save American motorists from their own stupidity, MG were forced to detune the MGB for the American market. As is often the case, legislation was being put in place by those ill advised to be making it. Many of the regulations being imposed were less for true safety aspects and more for the avoidance of litigation by motorists involved in accidents who were unwilling to take responsibility for their own actions. Other amendments to the design at this time were more in line with BL cost savings than the desire to create a better car. The traditional leather seats were replaced with heavy vinyl that would bond itself to the driver's skin on a hot day and the familiar wire spoke steering wheel was replaced with a mild steel version with drilled flat spokes; this, however, was soon dropped in favour of a slotted design after a police driver managed to trap his finger in one of the holes

thus immobilising himself and the car!

The slotted wheel was itself abandoned just one year later after the NHTSA decided that it posed a risk to wearers of rings and bracelets and was soon replaced by a similar design in which the slots had been filled. More significant legislation had been brought into place requiring that all vehicles be capable of withstanding a 5mph impact without damaging either the control or the safety systems. To conform to this, outsized and rather unattractive overriders were fitted to the front and rear bumpers. But this in itself was not good enough for some.

California, a state with a reputation for bad parking and setting its own agenda, stipulated that in a 5mph impact there should be no damage to the vehicle whatsoever. This was to have catastrophic implications for the sleek and beautiful MGB and its Midget stablemate. In order to comply with these additional requirements a substantial redesign was implemented that resulted in an additional 32kgs of steelwork being fitted to the front and rear of the car encased in black polyurethane mouldings that added 5" to the length of the car and did nothing for its looks whatsoever. In addition, further US legislation required that all motorvehicle bumpers should be fitted at a standard distance above the ground resulting in Abingdon's engineers having to increase the ride height by 1½". Whilst this may well have protected Californian consumers from bodywork damage inflicted by questionable parking techniques it did little for the car's handling. The once sorted sportster now found itself liable to body roll and a feeling of instability when cornering at speed. It was though not just the American purchasers on whom these modifications were inflicted. In line with the usual British Leyland frugality it was decided that the rubber bumper model MGs

would become the company standard. The cars would never be the same again.

There was, however, one small point of good fortune for MG buyers in the home market in that they were not subjected to the power restrictions imposed on the American models, once again due to draconian Californian legislature. To fall in line with emission regulations a small valve head and single Stromberg carburettor replaced the standard unit and twin SU carburettors with exhaust gases being subsequently fed through an early catalytic converter. Not only was the US market MG forced to carry a substantial weight penalty due to its hefty rubber-covered ironwork it was also subjected

to a 20bhp loss in power.

The body-roll issue was eventually addressed in 1976 by the fitment of an anti roll bar but further restrictive legislation was on the cards as a result of Brussels implementing the new EEC Type Approval Regulations. It soon became apparent that the days of the existing B-Series engine, although well modified from its original form, were well and truly numbered. Without extensive reworking there was no way in which it would be able to comply with the ever tightening requirements regarding safety and emissions. The Abingdon drawing office had been working for some time on the project but the fruit of their labours, the O-Series, was to live its life instead in the more mundane surroundings of the Morris Marina and Austin Princess engine compartments.

MG pressed on with production of the MGB and Midget despite it being thoroughly clear that both machines were now way past their respective sell by dates. The 1980s were approaching and they had been in production for the best part of 20 years with their origins stepping back even further; it was after all in 1951 that George Philips' special bodied Le Mans TD inspired the MGA and in turn the MGB designs. There were also new competitors in the market for the crown of affordable sportster: Triumph, a competitor from within the BL stable, had launched their wedge shaped TR7, and a new concept, the hot hatch, had been born overnight with the creation of the Volkswagen Golf GTi. There was no doubting that MG needed a new model and fast.

But funds were not forthcoming. British Leyland chairman, Sir Michael Edwardes, claimed that MG was just not profitable and that the company lost £900 for every car sold; this was despite the fact that the autonomous nature of BL had long since removed the responsibility of sourcing and sales

from the Abingdon plant and that every car built by the group lost money. The writing was on the wall and very soon an announcement was made that the factory was to be closed and the MG marque resigned to the pages of history.

This caused considerable uproar on both sides of the Atlantic. In the UK a mass protest was organised on the streets of London culminating in the handing over of a 12,246 signature petition at British Leyland's head office. In the US, the members of the Dealer Advisory Council offered to place an order for $200 million worth of cars. Even the House of Commons set up an MG Emergency Committee. But it was to no avail. First Midget production was suspended in late 1979 and the factory moved to a two-day working week producing a handful of MGBs, then, finally on 24 October 1980 the Abingdon plant's factory doors were bolted shut for ever.

It was the saddening end of an era, not just for MG but for the entire British motor industry.

BELOW South African-born business executive and newly appointed chairman of British Leyland, Michael Edwardes, outside Leyland's London Piccadilly offices

ASTON MARTIN

Through the ages

International
1929-1932

WHEN CESARE BERTELLI BECAME involved with Aston Martin, he wanted the company's cars to be reliable enough to take you from England to France, compete in the Le Mans 24-Hour race and then drive the car home again, all in comfort.

The road-going solution that he came up with was the International, so named because it was designed to comply with the regulations of the international motorsport governing body, AIACR (Association Internationale des Automobile Clubs Reconnus).

The car was powered by a 1.5-litre engine that had been designed by Claude Hill, who would go on to be responsible for the radical Atom. It was a simple, overhead camshaft unit that offered the required reliability and had dry-sump lubrication so it could be mounted low in the body. To optimise the car's handling, the chassis was under-slung to ensure a low centre of gravity, and to give the car a low and sporty appearance.

The majority of Internationals were two-seater, open-top cars, although a long-chassis version was offered which had room in the back for two passengers. There was also a very pretty fixed-head coupe that was built to special order – one of the advantages of a separate chassis was that it was relatively simple to fit custom-made bodywork.

In 1931, Aston Martin offered a more race-inspired version of the car, which was the International Le Mans (not to be confused with the later car that was called simply 'Le Mans'). This was mechanically similar to the standard car but had sleeker bodywork that was based on the company's team racecars of the period.

The following year, the International was heavily revised in an attempt to make it less expensive to produce. This was retrospectively known as the 'New International' and only about a dozen are believed to have been built. It had a new chassis design and a cheaper transmission system, and could be identified by its tapered radiator. Incidentally, the 'New International' was the first Aston Martin to feature the now famous winged badge, although it was dropped from the subsequent Le Mans model.

SPECIFICATION

Engine: Four inline cylinders with overhead camshaft
Capacity: 1494cc
Bore x stroke: 69x99mm
Maximum Power: 56bhp at 4250rpm
Maximum Torque: n/a
Transmission: Four-speed manual
Suspension: Front: Rigid axle with leaf springs. Rear: Live axle with leaf springs.
Length: 3900mm
Width: 1640mm
Height: 1300mm
Weight: 860kg
Top Speed: 75mph
0-60mph: n/a

Le Mans
1932-1933

ASTON MARTIN WAS STRUGGLING to make any money at the start of the 1930s, partly because of the poor economic climate and partly because its cars were expensive to produce and the com-

pany was going through a difficult time, with various investors coming and going.

The so-called New International of 1931 addressed the cost issue to some extent but was not a sales success, so a

new model was developed with which to tempt customers.

That new car was known as the Le Mans (not to be confused with the earlier International Le Mans) in deference to the company's ongoing success at the famous French endurance race.

Although mechanically similar, and with a same basic chassis, the Le Mans had restyled bodywork with a lower, squatter radiator that was designed to make the car push through the air more efficiently. The aerodynamics were also improved by a hood that folded flush with the bodywork – in those days, people drove with the roof down in all but the most inclement weather, even when racing – and, as before, the front cycle wings moved as the steering turned. The Le Mans was offered in two- and four-seater form; the latter with a longer chassis.

The engine of the Le Mans was essentially the same Claude Hill four-cylinder, 1.5-litre unit as used in the previous International. However, for the new car, it had been uprated with magnesium pistons, a higher compression ratio, twin electric fuel pumps (the driver could control which one was operating) and other refinements that upped the power to an extravagant (for its day) 70bhp, which was enough to drive the lightweight car at speeds of over 80mph.

Despite the best attempts of the company's engineers, the Le Mans ended up costing some £120 more than the equivalent International, at £595 in two-seater form. Bizarrely, though, it turned out to be a much more successful car for Aston Martin, with more than 100 examples being sold in 1932 and 1933. Just 15 of these were the long-wheelbase, four-seater cars.

SPECIFICATION

Engine: Four inline cylinders with overhead camshaft

Capacity: 1494cc

Bore x stroke: 69x99mm

Maximum Power: 70bhp at 4750rpm

Maximum Torque: n/a

Transmission: Four-speed manual

Suspension: Front: Rigid axle with leaf springs. Rear: Live axle with leaf springs

Length: 4050mm

Width: 1680mm

Height: 1230mm

Weight: 1020kg

Top Speed: 84mph

0-60mph: n/a

Mark II and Ulster

1934-1935

BY THE EARLY 1930S, ASTON MARTIN was owned by the Sutherland family and they were keen to make the company profitable. One solution they came up with was to broaden the marque's appeal by moving away from race-orientated cars, such as the Le Mans, and towards something rather more refined and sophisticated. Looking back, this was a decision that was going to have a long-term influence on future Aston Martins as this was the direction most models would take.

The first car to adopt this policy was the Mark II of 1934. This used essentially the same chassis as the Le Mans, albeit stiffened and fitted with a different front suspension to improve the road-holding somewhat.

The car was available in short and long wheelbase form, the latter with a reasonable amount of space for rear

passengers. The short wheelbase version was available only as an open-top car, while the long wheelbase could also be had in tourer and saloon body styles. The Mark II retained the squat radiator of the Le Mans but this time it was visually enhanced with smart vertical slats instead of mesh. This not only gave the car a classy appearance, the slats also opened and closed via a thermostat to control the air flow. As was by now an Aston Martin trademark, the front cycle wings moved with the steering.

The Mark II was powered by the same four-cylinder, 1.5-litre engine as used in the Le Mans, albeit slightly tweaked to produce 73bhp, and the power was fed to the rear wheels via a four-speed gearbox.

A racing car was developed from the Mark II and these proved very successful in competition, winning first, second and third in class at the 1934 Ulster Tourist Trophy. This led to a replica version, called the Ulster, being made for the public to buy.

The Ulster, of which just 21 were built, had a similar body to the race cars; low and narrow with a sleek boat-shaped tail that contained the spare wheel. Because previous Aston Martin racing cars had been painted British Racing Green and had been unlucky in competition, Cesare Bertelli, who was looking after the racing side of the business, decided to opt for bright red – the colour of his home country, Italy.

Crucially, the Ulster was guaranteed to reach the magical 100mph mark. This was made possible by way of a tuned version of the Mark II engine. A higher compression ratio (9.5:1), along with polished ports and larger SU carburettors, combined to push the maximum power output to 85bhp.

SPECIFICATION

Engine: Four inline cylinders with overhead camshaft
Capacity: 1494cc
Bore x stroke: 69x99mm
Maximum Power: 73bhp at 4750rpm
Maximum Torque: n/a
Transmission: Four-speed manual
Suspension: Front: Rigid axle with leaf springs. Rear: Live axle with leaf springs
Length: 3850mm
Width: 1630mm
Height: 1200mm
Weight: 870kg
Top Speed: 92mph
0-60mph: n/a

15/98

WITH THE 15/98 OF 1936, ASTON Martin moved even further from its sporting roots in an attempt to increase market share. The name referred to the engine's RAC taxable horsepower (15) and actual horsepower (98bhp). Respectable figures that were used in cars that were more high-speed tourers

than out and out sports cars.

The 15/98 was powered by a 2.0-litre four-cylinder engine that had been developed from the previous 1.5-litre unit, with the inlet and exhaust ports reversed to improve efficiency.

Styling-wise, the 15/98 was a very different car, indeed. Offered in short and long chassis versions, buyers could choose from open-top tourers, drophead coupes or a closed saloon. Gone were the previous cycle wings, to be replaced with more modern fixed front wings that swept back to meet the running boards, as was the fashion of the day. The rear wings aped the fronts and swept back into a streamlined rear panel.

It was undoubtedly an elegant car and one designed for touring rather than racing. Indeed, in four-door saloon form, there was very little sportiness about the 15/98; it was more of a luxury saloon, and not a particularly fast one because the four-cylinder engine had a lot of bodywork to move.

That said, the smaller, open versions of the 15/98 remained relatively sprightly and fun to drive, with a top speed of over 80mph.

There is no doubt that the 15/98 moved Aston Martin forward in terms of styling and market appeal. Unfortunately, though, the Second World War brought a halt to the company's development plans and, after the cessation of hostilities, the postwar Aston Martins would be very different animals altogether.

SPECIFICATION

Engine: Four inline cylinders with overhead camshaft
Capacity: 1950cc
Bore x stroke: 78x102mm
Maximum Power: 98bhp at 5000rpm
Maximum Torque: n/a
Transmission: Four-speed manual
Suspension: Front: Rigid axle with leaf springs. Rear: Live axle with leaf springs
Length: 4000mm
Width: 1590mm
Height: 1400mm
Weight: 1150kg
Top Speed: 83mph
0-60mph: n/a

Atom
1939

THE ATOM WAS A ONE-OFF PROtotype yet, as things turned out, it was one of the most important cars Aston Martin ever built. Why? Because it was after driving the Atom, that David Brown decided to buy Aston Martin in 1947, and its underpinnings went on to be the basis for the postwar DB range of production cars right up to 1958.

However, that was not the original plan. The Atom was planned as a production car and was the brainchild of Aston Martin designer, Claude Hill, and he used some revolutionary ideas. First, the car was built around a cage of square tubes (the so-called Superleggara principle that would go on to be the basis of later Aston Martins) onto which the aluminium body panels were attached.

And what a body it was! Hill's design stunned the prewar world, with its futuristic streamlined shape. The Atom was like no other car, its curvaceous lines hinted at a brave new world and its integrated front grille, low-mounted headlamps and long pointed bonnet looked powerful and aggressive. Oddly, despite the curved bodywork, all the glass on the car was flat, necessitating a split windscreen.

There was more to the Atom than just its space age appearance, though. Under the bonnet was a new four-cylinder, 2.0-litre engine designed by Hill himself (although, initially, the 15/98 engine was used). And this was linked to an exciting four-speed gearbox that was electromagnetically controlled – instead of a conventional gearlever, the driver selected gears using a small, dash-mounted controller.

The suspension was developed with the help of engineer, Gordon Armstrong, and consisted of a conventional live axle with leaf springs at the back, and independent trailing arms and coil springs up front.

It was an impressive package and one, if it had gone into production, that would have shaken up the staid motor industry of the time. Sadly, though, it was not to be, as the Second World War put paid to the plans and Aston Martin became involved in producing aircraft parts for the war effort.

However, Claude Hill didn't neglect his baby and continued to develop it in spare moments throughout the war. And then, when Aston Martin went up for sale, the by now scruffy-looking Atom was one of the company's few assets. David Brown took it home with him for a few days' driving and was so impressed, he bought the company. So if it hadn't been for the little Atom, Aston Martin – assuming it survived – would be a very different company and we wouldn't have had the DB range of cars.

SPECIFICATION

Engine: Four inline cylinders with twin SU carburettors

Capacity: 1970cc

Bore x stroke: 82.5x92mm

Maximum Power: 80bhp at 4760rpm

Maximum Torque: n/a

Transmission: Four-speed manual with electromagnetic control

Suspension: Front: Independent, trailing arms and coil springs. Rear: Live rear axle with trailing arms and leaf springs

Length: 4430mm

Width: 1540mm

Height: 1500mm

Weight: 1200kg

Top Speed: 102mph

0-60mph: n/a

2-Litre Sports ('DB1')

1948-1950

THE FIRST ASTON MARTIN PRO-duced under the directorship of David Brown was the 2-Litre Sports of 1948. Because of this, and the fact it was followed by the DB2, this rare car is often retrospectively known as the 'DB1', although it was never badged thus.

Because funds and time were tight, the 2-Litre Sports used as its basis the same tubular chassis as the prewar Atom, albeit lengthened and modified, and fitted with different suspension front and back.

The aluminium body was styled by Frank Feeley, who had previously been at Lagonda. It might not have been as radical as that of the Atom, but the shape was nonetheless modern, smooth and elegant. And, importantly, its distinctive grille would be the inspiration for all future Aston Martins, right up to

the present day. An unusual feature was a clever housing for the spare wheel within the left-hand front wing, while the rear wheel arches could be removed and replaced with flush panels to cover the tops of the wheels completely.

The car was a two-seater, but the bench seat did allow a third person to be squeezed in if required. The Sports was designed as a drop-head coupe, although a couple of examples were built with fixed roofs.

The 2-Litre Sports was powered by the 1970cc four-cylinder engine that Claude Hill had developed for the Atom, although this time it was linked to a conventional four-speed gearbox. The compact engine looked lost under that long bonnet and didn't give the car the performance it deserved but, at the time, it was the only powerplant available to the company.

A racing version of the 2-Litre Sports was also produced and became known as the 'Spa Special' because it won the legendary 24-hour race in 1948, driven by St John Horsfall and Leslie Johnson. This was great publicity for Aston Martin and did much to raise the profile of the marque around the world. Sadly, though, it was not enough to persuade many buyers in the austere postwar economy to buy a car that was more than twice the price of the contemporary Jaguar XK120, which did much the same job.

Indeed, in the event, Aston Martin only produced around 15 examples of the expensive 2-Litre Sports between 1948 and 1950, the majority being drophead coupes. It was then replaced by the more powerful and more refined DB2 with its six-cylinder engine.

SPECIFICATION

Engine: Four inline cylinders with twin SU carburettors

Capacity: 1970cc

Bore x stroke: 82.5x92mm

Maximum Power: 90bhp at 4750rpm

Maximum Torque: n/a

Transmission: Four-speed manual

Suspension: Front: Independent, trailing arms and coil springs. Rear: Live axle with coil springs

Length: 4470mm

Width: 1710mm

Height: 1410mm

Weight: 1145kg

Top Speed: 80mph

0-60mph: n/a

DB2
1950-1953

THE FIRST ASTON MARTIN TO carry a 'DB' badge was the DB2 which was first unveiled in 1950 and was promptly described as 'the most beautiful car in the world' by an enthusiastic Motor magazine.

And it truly was a wonderful-looking machine. Designer Frank Feeley created something that was way ahead of most other cars on the road in appearance and there was a hint of Italian styling in the DB2's flowing lines.

The body panels were hand-formed from lightweight 18-gauge aluminium and attached to a strong but light square-section tubular frame, which

was derived from that of the prewar Atom prototype. The bonnet and front wings were combined into one large panel that tipped forwards to give excellent access to the engine.

The engine itself was a straight-six unit designed by WO Bentley. It featured an iron block, twin overhead camshafts and had a capacity of 2580cc. Producing 105bhp at 5000rpm, it was a powerful unit for its day, and a top speed of 117mph was considered quite respectable.

SPECIFICATION

Engine: Six inline cylinders with twin overhead camshafts

Capacity: 2580cc

Bore x stroke: 78x90mm

Maximum Power: 105bhp at 5000rpm

Maximum Torque: 169Nm at 3000rpm

Transmission: Four-speed manual

Suspension: Front: Independent, trailing arms and coil springs. Rear: Live rear axle with trailing arms and coil springs

Length: 4130mm

Width: 1650mm

Height: 1360mm

Weight: 1111kg

Top Speed: 117mph

0-60mph: 11.2 seconds

The power was fed through a four-speed gearbox that was sourced, not surprisingly, from the David Brown Group and it had synchromesh on all gears.

The very early DB2s had three-piece front grilles but, on later cars, the three sections were merged into a single grille to give a cleaner design that would be aped in later Aston Martins.

The DB2 was available in coupe and drophead coupe forms, while a more powerful Vantage version followed at the end of 1950. This was also available in coupe and drophead coupe forms, and had a more powerful engine that produced 125bhp, thanks in part to larger twin SU carburettors.

Inside, the DB2 was strictly a two-seater car, with passengers enjoying a comfortable, leather-lined cockpit. Luggage space, however, was limited to a small area behind the seats. The small hatch that was accessed from the rear of the car was filled with the spare wheel.

The DB2 was an expensive car. In 1952 the coupe version cost £2724 in the UK, which was around £1000 more than the contemporary Jaguar XK120. Over its three-year production life, 411 examples of the DB2 were built, and about one-quarter of those were drophead coupes.

DB Mark III

1957-1959

THE DB2/4 MARK II WAS REPLACED by the DB Mark III, which was to be the final incarnation of the cars developed from Claude Hill's Atom chassis and with the Lagonda-based straight-six engine.

The car's name is rather confusing because you'd expect it to be called the DB3, but that name had already been used for a racecar, so the new road-going model was called DB Mark III, although it's often incorrectly referred to as the DB3.

The new car was an evolution of the

DB2/4 Mark II, but with a few small but noticeable changes to the body shape. At the front, the previously fussy grille was simplified and put in front of a new, elegantly curved bonnet. Out back, meanwhile, the tail-lights were replaced by slender vertical units. It was a simple restyle but enough to restore the elegance to the DB.

Inside, a much-needed new instrument cowl echoed the shape of the grille and gave Aston Martin a modern dash-board at long last. The useful hatchback and practical load space remained on the coupe versions.

The 3.0-litre straight-six engine had been reworked by Tadek Marek with a stiffer crankshaft, new block, new oil pump, larger valves, high-lift camshafts, a new exhaust system and much more. The result was an output of 162bhp at 5500rpm. An optional DBC engine came equipped with three Weber carburettors and was claimed to produce a heady 214bhp (just 14 cars were built with this engine). To cope with the extra power, all but the first 100 DB Mark IIIs were equipped with front Girling disc brakes instead of drums.

As before, the power went through a four-speed manual gearbox. However, in 1959 a Borg Warner automatic transmission became an option for the first time – a sign that Aston Martin was trying to widen its appeal – but only five cars were thus equipped in the end.

In its production life, a total of 551 DB Mark IIIs were built, of which 462 were coupes and 84 were drophead coupes. With its revamped engine, it was a far better car than the earlier DB2s and, as such, is much sought after today.

SPECIFICATION

Engine: Six inline cylinders with twin overhead camshafts

Capacity: 2922cc

Bore x stroke: 83x90mm

Maximum Power: 162bhp at 5000rpm

Maximum Torque: 195Nm at 3000rpm

Transmission: Four-speed manual

Suspension: Front: Independent, trailing arms and coil springs. Rear: Live rear axle with trailing arms and coil springs

Length: 4300mm

Width: 1650mm

Height: 1360mm

Weight: 1179kg

Top Speed: 120mph

0-60mph: 12.6 seconds

DB4
1958-1963

WORK BEGAN ON THE DB4 AT about the same time as the DB Mark III was being developed. The new car debuted at the 1958 London Motor Show and, in fact, the DB Mark III also continued in production for another year after.

The DB4 was essentially an all-new car. Gone was the long-serving square-tubed frame, to be replaced by a hefty sheet-steel floorpan with a tubular steel cage above, on which the hand-formed aluminium body panels were attached – a system called Superleggara. It was a strong and stiff construction, if a trifle over-engineered because of cost constraints.

The four-seater body was designed by the Italian Carrozzeria Touring company and drew inspiration from earlier DBs, but with a dash of Italian flair. In other words, it looked simply gorgeous and the DB4 remains, for many, the definitive Aston Martin.

Under that long bonnet with its purposeful air-scoop lay a new 3.7-litre, six-cylinder engine designed by Tadek Marek. Unlike the previous DB engine, this one had an all-alloy construction, thus saving weight. In standard form, this engine, that looked almost as good as the car, produced 240bhp at 5500rpm, while the Vantage version, which came later, was boosted to 266bhp at 5750rpm.

With this sort of power, the DB4 became the first production car to be capable of reaching 100mph and returning to a standstill in under 30 seconds – the 0-100mph time was cited at 21 seconds, while all-round disc brakes helped on the way back to zero. And with a 0-60mph time of 9.0 seconds and a heady top speed of 140mph, here was a machine that could compete with the best of the Italian supercars of the day.

The power was fed through a four-speed manual gearbox with the option of an overdrive, which made for more comfortable high-speed cruising. A Borg-Warner three-speed automatic

SPECIFICATION

Engine: Six inline cylinders with twin overhead camshafts
Capacity: 3670cc
Bore x stroke: 92x92mm
Maximum Power: 240bhp at 5500rpm
Maximum Torque: 325Nm at 4250rpm
Transmission: Four-speed manual with optional overdrive, or three-speed automatic
Suspension: Front: Independent, upper and lower A-arm and coil springs. Rear: Live rear axle with Watt linkage, trailing arms and coil springs
Length: 4480mm
Width: 1680mm
Height: 1310mm
Weight: 1296kg
Top Speed: 140mph
0-60mph: 9.0 seconds

was also optional.

Over its production life, the DB4 was revised and updated and there are five distinct versions, which are known as Series 1 to Series 5 (some of the last ones had the cowled headlamps from the DB4 GT and looked very similar to the DB5). A convertible version was also offered from 1961.

DB4 GT

1959-1963

A YEAR AFTER THE STUNNING NEW DB4 debuted, Aston Martin again wooed customers at the London Motor Show. This time with the DB4 GT. This was, though, much more than simply a more powerful incarnation with a 'GT' badge attached; it was a very different car in many ways.

The GT used the same Superleggera system as the standard DB4, with its tubular steel cage and steel floorpan under an aluminium body. However, the wheelbase was a full 130mm shorter and the car was now strictly a two-seater.

This was to improve the car's handling – especially on a racetrack – and it also served to make it lighter by about 80kg (that steel floorpan was relatively heavy compared to the body above).

The same basic body styling remained, albeit with smaller doors to suit the shortened wheelbase. At the front, though, appeared a new feature that would go on to be an Aston Martin trademark right through the 1960s – the headlamps were set back and covered with distinctive cowlings to aid aerodynamics.

The DB4 GT was powered by an uprated version of the DB4's all-alloy 3.7-litre engine. Twin sparkplugs per cylinder, triple Weber 45DCO carburettors and some other detail changes combined to boost power to no less than 302bhp at 6000rpm – an astonishing figure for its day.

The performance was no less astonishing, either. The DB4 GT, with its lighter body and more powerful engine, could shoot to 60mph in a blisteringly quick 6.4 seconds (that's still fast by today's standards) and go on to a top speed of 153mph. It's handling, too, was excellent, while uprated race-style brakes helped to cope with the extra power. In its day, the DB4 GT was pretty much unbeatable.

However, an even more powerful version, the DB4 GT Zagato appeared in 1960. This had a completely restyled body, from the Italian Zagato company, a race-style interior and a 314bhp engine. Only 19 examples of this expensive piece of exotica were built. However, in 1991, four more were built by Zagato.

SPECIFICATION

Engine: Six inline cylinders with twin overhead camshafts

Capacity: 3670cc

Bore x stroke: 92x92mm

Maximum Power: 302bhp at 6000rpm

Maximum Torque: 325Nm at 5000rpm

Transmission: Four-speed manual

Suspension: Front: Independent, upper and lower A-arm and coil springs. Rear: Live rear axle with Watt linkage, trailing arms and coil springs

Length: 4440mm

Width: 1680mm

Height: 1320mm

Weight: 1227kg

Top Speed: 153mph

0-60mph: 6.4 seconds

DB5

1963-1965

DB5 WAS AN EVOLUTION OF THE last of the DB4s that preceded it and went on to become perhaps the most famous Aston Martin of all time, after it appeared in the James Bond films Goldfinger and Thunderball in the early 1960s.

The new car was very similar in appearance to the DB4 Series 5, with the distinctive cowled headlamps that first appeared on the DB4 GT. Indeed, it was almost called the DB4 Series 6. As before, the body used a steel chassis with a unique tubular frame, on which the aluminium body panels were mounted. By making the car around 90mm longer, there was slightly more room inside, making it a more comfortable touring car. The downside was, though, that it was a heavier car.

However, it was under the bonnet

that the real changes occurred. The DB5's six-cylinder engine had an increased capacity, and was now 4.0-litres thanks to an increase in bore to 96mm. This led to a power output of 282bhp at 5500rpm in standard form. Unfortunately, though, the extra weight of the car pretty much negated the increase in power, so it wasn't until the Vantage version arrived, with its 314bhp at 5750rpm, that a real improvement in performance over the DB4 could be noticed.

As before, the standard four-speed gearbox could be supplemented with an optional overdrive. However, from 1964, the car was fitted with a new five-speed gearbox. A three-speed automatic remained an option but was rarely chosen.

Performance figures were impressive, with 60mph appearing in just 7.1 seconds and the DB5 going on to a top speed of 142mph.

Inside, the DB5 retained the distinctive instrument cowling that echoed the shape of the radiator grille, and this was filled with an array of dials. Leather and Wilton carpet ensured that the car was a comfortable and appealing place for two front passengers, plus two small ones in the back seats.

In its two-year production life, 886 DB5 coupes were built, plus 123 convertibles. There were also 12 shooting brakes, or estates, specially built to order by the Radford coachwork company.

SPECIFICATION

Engine: Six inline cylinders with twin overhead camshafts

Capacity: 3995cc

Bore x stroke: 95x92mm

Maximum Power: 282bhp at 5500rpm

Maximum Torque: 390Nm at 3850rpm

Transmission: Four-speed manual with optional overdrive (five-speed from 1964), or three-speed automatic

Suspension: Front: Independent, upper and lower A-arm and coil springs

Rear: Live rear axle with Watt linkage, trailing arms and coil springs

Length: 4570mm

Width: 1680mm

Height: 1320mm

Weight: 1466kg

Top Speed: 142mph

0-60mph: 7.1 seconds

DB6
1965-1970

ONCE AGAIN, THE DB6 WAS AN evolution of the previous model, the DB5, rather than an all-new car, although it did feature a number of changes.

Unveiled at the 1965 London Motor Show, under the skin, the DB6 moved away from the complex and expensive Superleggara construction and more towards a sheet-steel framework onto which the aluminium bodywork was attached.

That bodywork was restyled to ensure that the DB6 stood out from its predecessors. At the rear, the curved bootlid was replaced by a more modern and angular item with a neat built-in lip spoiler to aid aerodynamics. The rear side-windows, too, were reshaped with a thicker, more prominent C pillar. The front end, meanwhile, remained largely unchanged from that of the DB5, with its trademark Aston Martin grille (although a secondary grille appeared under the numberplate to feed air to the oil cooler).

The DB6 was 90mm longer than the DB5 and had a slightly higher roofline, thus improving the accommodation inside, especially for rear passengers. Apart from that and new front seats, the interior was much the same

SPECIFICATION

Engine: Six inline cylinders with twin overhead camshafts
Capacity: 3995cc
Bore x stroke: 95x92mm
Maximum Power: 282bhp at 5500rpm
Maximum Torque: 390Nm at 3850rpm
Transmission: Five-speed manual with optional overdrive or three-speed automatic
Suspension: Front: Independent, upper and lower A-arm and coil springs. Rear: Live rear axle with Watt linkage, trailing arms and coil springs
Length: 4620mm
Width: 1680mm
Height: 1360mm
Weight: 1474kg
Top Speed: 148mph
0-60mph: 6.1 seconds

as that of the DB5.

The engine, too, remained unchanged from the DB5 unit, being the now trusted straight-six, all-alloy 4.0-litre powerplant. The power was still 282bhp at 550rpm, although a Vantage version offered a worthwhile 325bhp. By now, the standard gearbox was a five-speed manual, while a three-speed automatic remained on the options list.

The DB6 was updated in 1969 and became the Mark II, although it was almost badged 'DB7'. This had lipped wheel arches, to accommodate wider wheels, whilst a small number were fitted with fuel injection, instead of carburettors.

The open-top DB6 was the first Aston Martin to carry the Volante name – the word is Italian for flying – although earlier convertibles are sometimes incorrectly referred to as such. As with the DB5, the Radford coachbuilding company made a small number of shooting brake or estate versions of the DB6.

DBS and DBS V8

1967-1972

WHEN ASTON MARTIN UNVEILED the all-new DBS at Blenheim Palace in Oxfordshire in 1967, it addressed the fact that the current DB6 was beginning to look dated – which was not surprising, considering it could trace its lineage back to the 1950s.

The DBS, on the other hand, was bang up to date, with its more angular lines, penned by William Towns, that would go on to form the mainstay of the Aston Martin line right into the 1980s. While the new car was very obviously an Aston Martin, it was larger and more aggressive than the DB6. At the front, the Aston Martin grille was cleverly reworked, to make it more integral with the bonnet line, and twin headlamps were set into the sides of the grille.

The chassis was essentially that of the DB6, albeit widened (by a noticeable 150mm) and lengthened. As ever, the bodywork was hand-formed from aluminium.

The DBS looked a mean muscle car but, unfortunately, under that huge bonnet lay the same six-cylinder engine from the DB6. In the larger car it gave adequate rather than earth-shattering performance. Aston Martin was working on a new V8 engine but it wasn't ready, which is why the six had to suffice.

By 1969, however, the new engine was

ready and was used in the DBS V8. With a capacity of 5.3 litres, twin overhead camshafts per cylinder bank and fuel injection, this beast of an engine produced 320bhp at 5000rpm and powered the DBS to 60mph in 6.0 seconds and on to a top speed of 160mph – not bad for a car that really could hold four people in comfort.

The six-cylinder variant continued to be offered alongside the V8 and, rather confusingly, went on to be badged 'Vantage' from 1972, even though that name was usually used for high-performance models. At the same time, the DBS badge was dropped from the V8-engined car and that then became known as the Aston Martin V8. This car remained in production, with only minor changes, into the 1980s.

SPECIFICATION - DBS

Engine: Six inline cylinders with twin overhead camshafts

Capacity: 3995cc

Bore x stroke: 95x92mm

Maximum Power: 282bhp at 5500rpm

Maximum Torque: 390Nm at 3850rpm

Transmission: Five-speed manual with optional overdrive or three-speed automatic

Suspension: Front: Independent, unequal wishbones and coil springs. Rear: De Dion axle with trailing arms, lever-arm dampers and coil springs

Length: 4580mm

Width: 1830mm

Height: 1330mm

Weight: 1588kg

Top Speed: 140mph

0-60mph: 7.1 seconds

SPECIFICATION - DBS V8

Engine: V8 cylinders with twin overhead camshafts

Capacity: 5340cc

Bore x stroke: 85x100mm

Maximum Power: 320bhp at 5500rpm

Maximum Torque: 542Nm at 4000rpm

Transmission: Five-speed manual with optional overdrive or three-speed automatic

Suspension: Front: Independent, unequal wishbones and coil springs.
Rear: De Dion axle with trailing arms, lever-arm dampers and coil springs

Length: 4580mm

Width: 1830mm

Height: 1330mm

Weight: 1727kg

Top Speed: 160mph

0-60mph: 6.0 seconds

Lagonda
1976-1989

THE ASTON MARTIN LAGONDA WAS unveiled in 1976 to an astonished world. There'd never been another car like it, and there never will be. It was conceived as a high-powered saloon car that would open up new markets for the company and, seeing that Aston Martin owned the Lagonda marque, it was decided to use that as a model name, rather than a brand – hence Aston Martin Lagonda.

The underpinnings were basically that of the DBS-based V8 of the day, so there was nothing particularly high-tech or revolutionary about that. However, it was the car's styling that created all the attention. The William Towns design was strikingly angular, with a long, low wedge-shaped bonnet (with a tiny Lagonda grille at the front) and there was hardly a curve to be seen.

The interior, too, was ahead of its time. Inside of traditional dials, the dashboard was equipped with space-age LED displays, touch-sensitive controls and a single-spoke steering wheel. In contrast, there were also acres of leather and wood, as befitted a luxury car.

Under that slender bonnet lay the 5.3-litre

V8 engine from the company's other cars, and this was equipped with Weber carburettors and linked to a crude and power-sapping Chrysler three-speed gearbox.

Although it was first shown in 1976, it wasn't until 1979 that the first Lagondas were delivered to eager customers. Over the years it was in production, it received a number of updates. The LED dashboard proved troublesome so in 1984 it was replaced with one that featured cathode ray tube displays, but these turned out to be just as unreliable, so vacuum fluorescent instruments were used from 1987. In the same year, the razor-sharp lines were softened slightly and the original pop-up headlamps were replaced by an array of three square lamps each side of the grille. The engine was also revised over the years, with the output reaching 300bhp.

In all, a total of 645 Lagondas were built and it proved particularly popular in the Middle East, which took about 30 percent of the total production of these expensive, hand-built status symbols. There was also a small number of long wheelbase Tickford Limousines that boasted colour televisions in the front and the back, while a Swiss company produced a shooting brake version.

The Aston Martin Lagonda was quietly dropped from the range at the end of the 1980s. It remains a unique car and very much a product of the 1970s. Some people think it's ugly and tacky, while others love the fact that it's so different from anything else on the roads. Whatever, there is no doubt that it will always remain a head-turner!

SPECIFICATION

Engine: V8 cylinders with twin overhead camshafts

Capacity: 5340cc

Bore x stroke: 85x100mm

Maximum Power: 280bhp at 5000rpm

Maximum Torque: 488Nm at 3000rpm

Transmission: Three-speed automatic

Suspension: Front: Independent, unequal wishbones and coil springs. Rear: De Dion axle with trailing arms, self-levelling dampers and coil springs

Length: 5283mm

Width: 1816mm

Height: 1302mm

Weight: 2064kg

Top Speed: 148mph

0-60mph: 7.9 seconds

V8 Vantage
1977-1989

AFTER THE DBS V8 BECAME KNOWN simply as the V8, it remained in production and a high-power variant was developed for 1977. Following the odd situation where the 'Vantage' badge was used on the entry-level six-cylinder model at the start of the 1970s, this time it reverted to its rightful place – on Aston Martin's flagship model.

The V8 Vantage used essentially the same bodyshell that dated back to the DBS of the 1960s, but was revised with new aerodynamic aids to help high-speed handling and to make the car look somewhat more modern and more aggressive. The previously open-fronted bonnet scoop became a closed power bulge in the bonnet, while the trademark Aston Martin radiator grille was blanked off and held two circular spotlights. Underneath this was a deep front spoiler with an air intake within it, while out back there was also a pronounced boot spoiler.

However, the main reason for the Vantage was to be found lurking under that purposeful bonnet bulge. The 5.3-litre V8 engine was breathed on to make

it even more powerful. Indeed, Aston Martin claimed a 40 percent increase in power and a 10 percent increase in torque over the standard car's engine. This was achieved by adapting an engine that had already appeared in the Nimrod racecar. Compared to the standard V8, this unit had revised camshafts, new intake system and manifolds, larger inlet valves, four twin-barrel Weber carburettors and different spark plugs.

SPECIFICATION

Engine: V8 cylinders with twin overhead camshafts

Capacity: 5340cc

Bore x stroke: 85x100mm

Maximum Power: 380bhp at 6600rpm

Maximum Torque: 552Nm at 4000rpm

Transmission: Five-speed manual

Suspension: Front: Independent, unequal wishbones and coil springs. Rear: De Dion axle with trailing arms, lever-arm dampers and coil springs

Length: 4665mm

Width: 1890mm

Height: 1325mm

Weight: 1820kg

Top Speed: 170mph

0-60mph: 5.3 seconds

The result was a beast of an engine that, in initial form, produced a healthy 380bhp at 6000rpm and propelled the big supercar to 60mph in 5.3 seconds and on to a top speed of 170mph. The only downside, perhaps, was an average fuel consumption figure of 11 miles per gallon! The power was fed through a five-speed manual gearbox, while the suspension, brakes and wheels were all uprated accordingly.

The V8 Vantage remained in production until 1989, by which time the engine power had risen to 438bhp at 6000rpm, thanks to fuel injection and other changes, and top speed was close to 190mph. By this time, though, the design was really beginning to show its age (remember that it dated back to the DBS of the late 1960s) and very few of these large and expensive cars were built in the model's final years.

V8 Volante

1978-1989

DURING THE MID-1970S IT WAS thought that open-top cars would be outlawed in the USA on safety grounds, so many car manufacturers stopped developing them at this period, preferring to concentrate on coupes.

As it turned out, though, the feared legislation did not happen and the buyers continued to demand open-top cars – especially Americans, who were keenly buying up older Aston Martin Volantes and the like, to enjoy in the sunny climates of places like California and Florida.

Aston Martin quickly rose to the challenge and produced an open version of its large V8 model, which was aimed squarely at the US market, which took much of the production. The new model was called the V8 Volante and used essentially the same body as the coupe, albeit stiffened to make up for the lack of a solid roof and fitted with a restyled bonnet. The elegantly styled hood raised and lowered at the touch of a button, after two catches were undone at the front, using an electro-hydraulic mechanism, and was fully lined to ensure quiet and refined high-speed motoring.

The interior of the V8 Volante was similar to that of the coupe but was enhanced with burr-walnut trim for extra opulence (a feature that didn't come to the coupe until later). The rear seats remained, making it one of the few open-top cars of the time that four people could enjoy in comfort.

The Volante was also offered with the more powerful Vantage engine, and this car was known, not surprisingly perhaps, as the V8 Vantage Volante.

By the mid-1980s, Aston Martin attempted to update the lines of the V8 Volante by endowing it with front and rear spoilers and sideskirts, similar to those used on the closed Vantage. Unfortunately, though, this was not a successful look and the car was criticised for looking rather tasteless – Prince Charles, when he ordered one, sensibly asked for the bodykit to be omitted from his car.

Around 900 V8 Volantes were built during its long 11-year production run (which compares to 2658 coupes) of which many went to the USA.

SPECIFICATION

Engine: V8 cylinders with twin overhead camshafts

Capacity: 5340cc

Bore x stroke: 85x100mm

Maximum Power: 380bhp at 6600rpm

Maximum Torque: 552Nm at 4000rpm

Transmission: Five-speed manual

Suspension: Front: Independent, unequal wishbones and coil springs. Rear: De Dion axle with trailing arms, lever-arm dampers and coil springs

Length: 4585mm

Width: 1890mm

Height: 1370mm

Weight: 1791kg

Top Speed: 150mph

0-60mph: 6.3 seconds

Bulldog

1980

AFTER DESIGNER WILLIAM TOWNS shocked the motoring world with the Aston Martin Lagonda of 1976, he came back and did it all over again in 1980, with the astonishing Bulldog concept car.

It was very obvious that the Bulldog came from the same pen as the Lagonda – its low, angular wedge shape was a dead give-away. However, the Bulldog – which stood just over one-metre tall – pushed the boundaries even further with massive, power-operated, gullwing doors, a single 60cm-long wiper blade, and a front 'bonnet' panel that dropped away to reveal an array of five headlamps. It was a striking car but took little, if any, inspiration from Aston Martin's illustrious past.

Another break with tradition was the car's layout – the engine was mid-mounted. This was – and still is – the preferred configuration for supercars but Aston Martin always pre-

ferred – and still does – to have the engine mounted at the front, driving the rear wheels. The advantage of a mid engine is that it makes the car well-balanced which can help high-speed handling.

The engine itself was a 5.3-litre V8 unit fitted with twin Garrett turbochargers and fuel injection, which was claimed to produce as much as 700bhp, although 650bhp was a more realistic output.

SPECIFICATION

Engine: V8 cylinders with twin Garrett turbochargers

Capacity: 5344cc

Bore x stroke: n/a

Maximum Power: circa 650bhp at 6000rpm

Maximum Torque: circa 670Nm at 5500rpm

Transmission: Five-speed manual

Suspension: Front: Independent with wishbones and coil springs

Rear: Independent with trailing arms and coil springs

Length: 4270mm

Width: 1918mm

Height: 1092mm

Weight: 1730kg

Top Speed: 191mph

0-60mph: 5.2 seconds

The reason for such a powerful engine was that the Bulldog was designed to break the magical 200mph barrier. The car was taken to the MIRA test ground where it was driven at a maximum speed of 191mph before unwanted lift forced the driver to back off. With further development it's likely that 200mph would have been possible

The interior of the Bulldog was just as exciting. The two-seater cockpit boasted digital displays and touch-sensitive controls, as seen in the Lagonda. In contrast, though, there was also Connolly leather, Wilton carpet and even walnut, on display in the well-appointed interior.

The Bulldog was a stunning machine and would have been a true supercar, if it had gone into production; at one point it was planned to produce a limited edition of about 25 cars. But that didn't happen; just the one example was built and this was sold to a private buyer soon after the 1980 launch. It was taken to the USA where it was repainted from silver and grey to metallic green, the fuel injection was replaced with Weber carburettors and other minor changes were made.

V8 Zagato
1986-1988

THE MID-1980S WAS the time of limited production supercars, with Porsche offering the 959 and Ferrari the 288 GTO. These were both high-tech cars that were, more often than not, bought by speculators rather than true enthusiasts, because there was a buoyant market for such exotica.

Aston Martin was quick to cash in on this, but didn't have the resources to compete with Porsche and Ferrari to produce a technologically advanced machine. Instead, it relied on good old-fashioned brute power and the adoption of a famous name – Zagato. This Italian styling firm had penned the Aston Martin DB4 GT Zagato in the early 1960s and this car was a sought-after collectors' item, so it made sense to milk this connection.

The new V8 Zagato was based on a shortened (by 406mm) version of the current V8's chassis. This was then clad in a rather angular and dumpy aluminium body, that was certainly distinctive but drew little on previous Aston Martins, save a stylised and squared-off front grille. The twin headlamps were set back under clear covers – a nod to the original DB4GT Zagato, perhaps.

The bonnet was punctuated by a massive bulge which was not part of the original design but proved necessary when it was decided to equip the V8 engine with 50mm Weber downdraught carburettors. The original plan was to use the standard engine from the V8 Vantage which, by this time, was fuel injected, but Aston Martin wanted to advertise the V8 Zagato as having at least 400bhp, and the only affordable way to do that was to use carburettors.

In the event, the engine was honed to such an extent that it developed no less than 432bhp at 6200rpm. Another reason for this power was that it was hoped that the car would hit the magical 300kmh mark (that's 186mph) and reach 60mph in less than five seconds. In the event, it was clocked at 299kmh, which was considered close enough! The 0-60mph dash, however, did come in as hoped, at just 4.8 seconds.

They were impressive figures for a car that lacked the turbochargers, fuel injection and even the ABS brakes which were essential requirements of the V8 Zagato's competitors.

Inside, the V8 Zagato's occupants were cosseted with leather and walnut, plus a well-equipped dashboard that was as angular as the car's exterior.

Just 52 examples of the V8 Zagato were built. However, there were also an additional 37 open-top Volante versions. As well as the folding roof, these also differed in that they had a less powerful engine with fuel injection and so didn't have the unsightly bonnet bulge.

SPECIFICATION

Engine: V8 cylinders with twin overhead camshafts
Capacity: 5340cc
Bore x stroke: 85x100mm
Maximum Power: 432bhp at 6200rpm
Maximum Torque: 535Nm at 5100rpm
Transmission: Five-speed manual
Suspension: Front: Independent wishbones and coil springs. Rear: De Dion axle with Watt linkage, trailing arms, lever-arm dampers and coil springs
Length: 4390mm
Width: 1860mm
Height: 1295mm
Weight: 1650kg
Top Speed: 185mph
0-60mph: 4.8 seconds

Virage
1988-1995

BY THE END OF THE 1980S, THE Aston Martin product range consisted of the now very dated V8 cars, which could trace their origins back to the 1960s and were looking very old-fashioned indeed. A new model was desperately needed, but there wasn't the money to invest in anything too radical.

Instead, the new car used as its base a shortened and modified Lagonda chassis onto which was mounted a stylish new body designed by John Heffernan and Ken Greenley. The new car appeared less bulky and less aggressive-looking than its predecessor and – perhaps unfortunately if you knew – was fitted with Volkswagen headlamps and rear lamps. On the whole, though, the design worked and was a successful reinterpretation of the classic Aston Martin lines for the 1980s and beyond. As before, the body was hand-made from aluminium by craftsman at the Newport Pagnell factory.

Power came from essentially the same V8 engine but one that had been thoroughly reworked by the American company, Calloway Engineering. The most noticeable change to the 5.3-litre engine was the adoption of all-new cylinder heads with four valves per cylinder, that allowed the use of unleaded fuel while, at the same time, maintaining power and improving economy.

In its initial form, the Virage engine produced 330bhp. However, in 1992, a 6.3-litre version came out and, by 1993, this engine was producing no less than 465bhp, thus addressing earlier criticisms that the original Virage was underpowered. By this time, the car's smooth lines were joined by flared wheel arches and larger front and rear spoilers. Also, ABS was available as an option for the first time on an Aston Martin.

The Virage interior was unashamedly luxurious because, by this time, wealthy buyers wanted to be pampered and Aston Martins had become known as luxury cars rather than pure sporting machines. There was, though, among all the leather and walnut, a sprinkling of Ford switchgear and other parts, which distracted a little from the overall effect. However, the good news was that the car was quieter and more comfortable than the previous model.

The Virage was also available in open-top Volante form from 1990, albeit with a slightly less powerful engine. Oddly, this was initially planned as a two seater but, by the time it went into production, it had the same four seats as the coupe version.

Although the Virage name was dropped in 1995, the same basic body design continued up until 2000, badged simply as 'V8'.

SPECIFICATION

Engine: V8 cylinders with twin overhead camshafts

Capacity: 5340cc

Bore x stroke: 85x100mm

Maximum Power: 330bhp at 6000rpm

Maximum Torque: 474Nm at 3700rpm

Transmission: Five-speed manual or three-speed automatic

Suspension: Front: Independent, transverse unequal wishbones and coil springs
Rear: De Dion axle with trailing arms, Watts linkage and coil springs

Length: 4735mm

Width: 1854mm

Height: 1321mm

Weight: 1790kg

Top Speed: 155mph

0-60mph: 5.8 seconds

Vantage
1992-2000

first time that an Aston Martin had been named simply 'Vantage', rather than the moniker being used as an amendment of another name.

The Vantage used essentially the same chassis as the Virage, albeit substantially modified to make it lighter and to improve handling. The hand-made aluminium body also looked very similar to that of the Virage, yet Aston Martin claimed that only the roof and the door skins were carried over from that car. The rest of the bodywork was new and flared wings, front and rear, gave the Vantage a wider, more aggressive and purposeful appearance.

The front of the Vantage retained the trademark Aston Martin grille, which was actually more defined than on the Virage, while the Virage's square headlamps (which were actually Volkswagen Corrado items) were replaced by clusters of three small,

THE VANTAGE WAS LAUNCHED AT the 1992 Birmingham Motor Show as Aston Martin's new flagship model. Apart from the short-lived DBS-bodied Vantage of the early 1970s, this was the

square lamps hidden behind clear plastic covers. The rear lights, meanwhile, were four round units. There were also side air-vents behind the front wheels, a deep front spoiler, sideskirts and an integral rear spoiler. The overall effect was that of a supercar that certainly meant business!

And that business was lurking under the long bonnet. The trusty 5.3-litre V8 engine from the Virage was endowed

SPECIFICATION

Engine: V8 cylinders with twin overhead camshafts and twin Eaton superchargers

Capacity: 5340cc

Bore x stroke: 85x100mm

Maximum Power: 3550bhp at 6500rpm

Maximum Torque: 745Nm at 4000rpm

Transmission: Six-speed manual

Suspension: Front: Independent, transverse unequal wishbones and coil springs

Rear: De Dion axle with trailing arms, Watts linkage and coil springs

Length: 4745mm

Width: 1920kg

Height: 1330mm

Weight: 1920kg

Top Speed: 186mph

0-60mph: 4.6 seconds

with a pair of Eaton superchargers – turbocharging was considered but dismissed because of the associated problems with turbo-lag. The result was a maximum power output of no less than 550bhp at 6500rpm, combined with a torque figure of 745Nm.

Fed through a six-speed manual gearbox, this was enough to propel the big car to 60mph in a mere 4.6 seconds and on to a top speed of 186mph. This really was an astonishing motorcar! However, there was more to come in 1998, when a 600bhp version was introduced.

The Vantage had essentially the same interior as the Virage, with four seats and plenty of leather and walnut to remind occupants that they were in a very special car, indeed.

The Vantage was very much a bespoke car that was built in very small numbers. Indeed, between 1992 and 2000, just 280 examples were built, in both coupe and open-top Volante forms. The last of the line were badged 'Le Mans' and featured blanked-out radiator grilles, a larger front spoiler, cooling ducts in the bonnet and different vents in the front wings. The owner's handbook even included directions to the Le Mans circuit!

DB7
1994-1999

THE FIRST ASTON MARTIN TO BE produced under Ford's ownership was the DB7, which appeared in 1994 and really was a thing of beauty. It was conceived as a spiritual successor to the DB4 and, therefore, smaller and lighter than the big V8s that preceded it. And, crucially, it would have a straight-six engine, just like the DB4, albeit a more powerful and refined powerplant. This concept of a smaller, less expensive, higher volume Aston Martin had originally been mooted by Victor Gauntlett and was instrumental in the sale of the company to Ford.

To keep costs down, the engine was, in fact, based on that previously used in the Jaguar XJ40. It was a light alloy, twin camshaft, straight-six, with a capacity of 3228cc. The cylinder head featured four valves per cylinder with Zytec electronic multi-point fuel injection, while the air needed to combust the fuel was delivered by a water-cooled Roots-type,

supercharger, which was driven by a toothed belt from the camshaft.

As it was, the Jaguar connection went much deeper, much to the annoyance of some purists. The DB7's chassis was based on that of the old XJS, while the car was built in the factory at Bloxham in Oxfordshire that had been used for the XJ220 supercar.

What's more, the DB7's designer, Ian Callum, had worked on the XJ220, as well. Callum was shown a DB4 and DB6 and asked to come up with a modern interpretation of them. And that's just what he did. He ignored the larger V8 cars, feeling that they were not in the true spirit of the marque, and came up with a pure design that was immediately recognisable as an Aston Martin and had clear links with the DB4 and DB6. What the new car wasn't, though, was a pastiche or a retro car – it was strikingly modern and forward thinking in its appearance.

Inside, too, the DB7 embraced Aston Martin values. In other words, there was plenty of leather and wood on show, and the cockpit was comfortable and luxurious, with two seats in the back that were ideal for children. OK, so some of the switchgear was derived from Ford, but at least it worked properly.

The DB7 was developed on a very tight budget and in a short timescale, yet remains to this day one of the best-looking cars ever built. It relaunched Aston Martin onto the world market – it sold in no less than 29 different countries – and proved to be a practical and enjoyable sportscar with a timeless appeal.

SPECIFICATION

Engine: Six cylinders inline with twin overhead camshafts, four valves per cylinder and supercharger

Capacity: 3239cc

Bore x stroke: 91x83mm

Maximum Power: 335bhp at 5500rpm

Maximum Torque: 500Nm at 3000rpm

Transmission: Four-speed automatic or five-speed manual

Suspension: Front: Independent, double wishbones and coil springs. Rear: Independent, lower wishbones with upper halfshaft links and coil springs

Length: 4631mm

Width: 1830mm

Height: 1238mm

Weight: 1725kg

Top Speed: 165mph

0-60mph: 5.8 seconds (manual transmission)

DB7 Vantage
1999-2003

AS GOOD AS THE ORIGINAL SIX-cylinder DB7 had been, there was a demand for a more powerful and more refined powerplant. And that car came along in 1999.

The DB7 Vantage replaced the original six-cylinder model and was powered by a new V12 engine – it was the first time a V12 had been fitted in an Aston Martin.

The engine was developed by Aston Martin with the help of Ford and Cosworth. The all-alloy unit was not much heavier than the original straight-six and boasted 48 valves and a capacity of 5935cc (commonly rounded up to 6.0-litres). Visteon EEC V engine management controlled the fuel injection, ignition and diagnostic systems.

This gave a maximum power output of 420bhp – a useful 85bhp more than the old engine – and it was delivered with a silky smoothness but – and this is the crucial point – the exhaust note remained aggressive and purposeful, as you'd expect of an Aston Martin.

There was, though, much more to the Vantage than a new engine. Aston Martin had spent two years listening to customers and exhaustively testing prototypes. More than 500,000 test miles were covered in temperatures ranging from -30°C to +45°C in Europe and North America, including an accelerated high-speed durability test of 48 hours continuous running at 165mph in Southern Europe in mid-summer temperatures.

In Britain a series of pre-production models of the DB7 Vantage were subjected to continuous 30-day accelerated durability tests – each equivalent to 100,000 miles of regular driving, at speeds of up to 140mph.

SPECIFICATION

Engine: V12 cylinders with four overhead camshafts and four valves per cylinder

Capacity: 5935cc

Bore x stroke: 89x79.5mm

Maximum Power: 420bhp at 6000rpm

Maximum Torque: 540Nm at 5000rpm

Transmission: Five-speed automatic or six-speed manual

Suspension: Front: Independent, double wishbones and coil springs

Rear: Independent, lower wishbones with upper halfshaft links and coil springs

Length: 4666mm

Width: 1830mm

Height: 1238mm

Weight: 1780kg

Top Speed: 185mph

0-62mph: 5.0 seconds (manual transmission)

The test cycles included regular passage through mud and salt baths, driving deliberately into traffic island kerbstones at 50mph and a series of fierce stop-start acceleration and brake tests. Body chassis components were tested to the limit over corrugated and ladder frame surfaces and specially engineered tracks littered with potholes and strategically placed concrete blocks.

The suspension and brakes were revised to cope with the extra power, while the transmission was upgraded to a new six-speed manual, with the option of a five-speed automatic.

The body was restyled, too, with a more aggressive front end, with larger air intakes and big round driving lights on each quarter.

The original DB7 was a great car, but the V12 Vantage made it even better. It did, though, take the concept a little away from the original roots of the DB4 and DB6, which were powered by straight-six engines.

Vanquish
2001-2006

THE VANQUISH WAS ASTON Martin's first flagship car of the 21st century, hand-built at the Newport Pagnell factory and, as such, was suitably state-of-the-art.

The large, curvaceous body was designed by Ian Callum and made use of exciting new technology to ensure a strong, stiff and light structure.

The main body structure, including the floor and the front and rear bulkheads was formed from extruded alu-minium sections bonded and riveted around the carbon fibre transmission tunnel. Single-piece composite inner body side sections with carbon fibre windscreen pillars were then bonded to the central structure.

At the front, a steel, aluminium and carbon fibre subframe carried the engine, transmission and front suspension. The front end incorporated deformable composite panels to provide crash protection and there was a similar

structure at the rear.

The underside of the car was completely flat to aid high-speed aerodynamics.

All the exterior panels, including the roof, bonnet, boot lid, front and rear wings and doors were produced from 'super-plastic-formed' and pressed aluminium. However, each individual

SPECIFICATION

Engine: V12 cylinders with four overhead camshafts and four valves per cylinder

Capacity: 5935cc

Bore x stroke: 89x79.5mm

Maximum Power: 460bhp at 6500rpm

Maximum Torque: 542Nm at 5000rpm

Transmission: Six-speed manual with Auto Shift Manual/Select Shift Manual (ASM/SSM) electro-hydraulic control system

Suspension: Front: Independent, double wishbones and coil springs

Rear: Independent, double wishbones with upper halfshaft links and coil springs

Length: 4665mm

Width: 1923mm

Height: 1238mm

Weight: 1835kg

Top Speed: 190mph

0-62mph: 5.0 seconds

panel was then tailored and bonded to the central structure by hand to ensure a perfect fit and finish.

Under that long bonnet lay essentially the same 6.0-litre V12 engine used in the DB7 Vantage, but uprated to produce no less than 460bhp and 542Nm of torque and linked to a drive-by-wire throttle system. The power went through a close-ratio, six-speed manual transmission that boasted Formula One-style finger-tip controls. These allowed clutchless gearchanges to be made in less than 250 milliseconds. Furthermore, the gearbox could be set to make fully automatic changes when desired.

All this ensured superb performance, with 62mph coming up in just five seconds and the car going on to a top speed of 190mph – the Vanquish was a true supercar.

The Vanquish had a refreshingly modern interior, with aluminium and carbon 5fibre replacing the traditional Aston Martin wood. However, there was still plenty of high-quality leather and Wilton carpet to cosset the lucky inhabitants. The car was offered with a choice of just two seats, with a luggage space behind, or four seats, with the rears being ideal for children.

DB7 Zagato
2002-2003

ASTON MARTIN FIRST WORKED with the Italian styling company, Zagato in 1961, when the two companies produced the DB4GT Zagato. Then, in 1987 came the V8 Zagato. So, it was not altogether surprising when it was announced that the two companies would collaborate once more on an exciting new project.

That was to become the DB7 Zagato. Based, as the name suggests, on the V12-engined DB7, the new car used some of the styling cues of the original DB4GT Zagato (the 1980s version was ignored) to produce a stunning interpretation for the 21st century.

The extra-large front grille was a Zagato trademark, as were the long bonnet, chopped tail, curvaceous rear arches and 'double bubble' roofline. The bodyshell was hand-made in Italy from aluminium with a steel roof and used a shortened DB7 Vantage Volante chassis. It was assembled in the UK at Aston Martin's Bloxham plant.

The powertrain remained standard DB7 fare, with the 6.0-litre V12 engine producing 420bhp. However, because the shortened aluminium was a full 60kg lighter than the standard car, it gave the Zagato a performance advantage. This was further enhanced by revised gear and differential ratios (it was available with a six-speed manual transmission only). The brakes and suspension were also uprated to give enhanced, sportier handling.

Zagato designed unique wheels for the car, which were 18 inches in diameter and had different offsets to give the DB7 Zagato a wider track to ensure the wheels filled the wider arches.

Inside, the Zagato interior was based on that of the standard DB7, but had a trimmed luggage shelf in place of the rear seats. The door trims were revised to suit the higher waist line, while the seats were trimmed in unique quilted leather with a Zagato 'Z' on the back of each.

Just 99 examples of the DB7 Zagato were built between 2002 and 2003, and they sold for around £160,000 each. They were offered in just three standard colours; Mercury Grey, Aqua Verde and Zagato Nero, while the leather interior was Dark Chocolate aniline leather.

SPECIFICATION

Engine: V12 cylinders with four overhead camshafts and four valves per cylinder
Capacity: 5935cc
Bore x stroke: 89x79.5mm
Maximum Power: 420bhp at 6000rpm
Maximum Torque: 540Nm at 5000rpm
Transmission: Six-speed manual
Suspension: Front: Independent, double wishbones and coil springs
Rear: Independent, lower wishbones with upper halfshaft links and coil springs
Length: 4481mm
Width: 1830mm
Height: 1244mm
Weight: 1740kg
Top Speed: 190mph
0-62mph: 4.9 seconds

DB American Roadster 1
2003-2004

although Aston Martin was at pains to stress that it was, in fact, a model in its own right.

Indeed, it had a very different (and, it has to be said, rather clumsy) name – DB American Roadster 1, or DB AR1. This set it apart from the Zagato and made it clear that the car was designed specifically to appeal to American customers.

Despite this, it was clear that the DB AR1 was very much based on the coupe Zagato and shared the same styling, front and back. The main difference, of course, was the lack of a roof. Indeed, the car

FOLLOWING ON FROM THE DB7 Zagato, Aston Martin and the famous Italian design company collaborated once more on another project. This was an open-top version of the Zagato – had no form of roof whatsoever, not even a folding soft-top – making it a roadster in the truest sense of the word, and only suitable for fair climes, such as California.

Like the Zagato, the bodyshell was hand-made in Italy and was mainly aluminium. Behind the seats were two distinctive humps, which echoed the 'double bubble' roof of the coupe.

Unlike the Zagato, though, the DB AR1 was equipped with an uprated version of the 6.0-litre V12 engine that produced no less than 435bhp at 6000rpm – up a worthwhile 15bhp from the standard 420bhp unit, while torque increased from 540Nm to 556Nm at 5000rpm. The exhaust system, meanwhile, had bypass valves in the rear silencers to give a sportier note.

The power went through an AP twin-plate racing clutch and a six-speed manual gearbox with revised ratios. To suit the target American market, a five-speed automatic gearbox was available as an option.

Brakes were upgraded, too, with racing-style grooved 355mm (front) and 330mm (rear) Brembo discs and Pagid RS 42-1 front pads. An uprated brake booster unit – as used on the V12 Vanquish – assisted in providing the driver with progressive braking and a firmer and more consistent pedal feel.

Zagato designed unique, lightweight alloy wheels for the DB AR1 that were 19 inches in diameter and had revised offsets to suit the wider wheel arches.

The DB AR1 interior was based on that of the standard DB7 but was uniquely trimmed in Bridge of Weir leather.

Just 99 examples of the DB AR1 were built in 2003 to 2004 and they were eagerly snapped up by collectors, hoping for a good long-term investment.

SPECIFICATION

Engine: V12 cylinders with four overhead camshafts and four valves per cylinder

Capacity: 5935cc

Bore x stroke: 89x79.5mm

Maximum Power: 435bhp at 6000rpm

Maximum Torque: 556Nm at 5000rpm

Transmission: Six-speed manual or five-speed automatic

Suspension: Front: Independent, double wishbones and coil springs

Rear: Independent, lower wishbones with upper halfshaft links and coil springs

Length: 4481mm

Width: 1830mm

Height: 1229mm

Weight: 1730kg

Top Speed: 190mph

0-62mph: 4.8 seconds

DB7 GT
2003-2004

THE DB7 REALLY WENT OUT WITH a bang before it was replaced with the all-new DB9. The DB7 GT was the last of the line and the most powerful DB7 ever, with its V12 tweaked to produce a full 435bhp (up from the standard 420bhp).

However, the increase in power was only part of the story. Aston Martin made the GT a more sporty car to drive than the standard DB7. Not only was there more mid-range torque from the uprated engine, the GT also had a revised final-drive ratio with limited-slip differential, active sports exhaust, a quick-shift gearchange and a racing twin-plate clutch (on manual transmission cars).

To make the DB7 really stand out, it received some subtle styling changes that,

not only made the car look more sporty and purposeful, also improved its aerodynamics, especially at high speed.

Under the car, the undertray was revised to improve downforce, as were the wheel arch liners. Combined with a lip spoiler on the bootlid, these reduced lift by almost 50 percent – useful when you're heading towards the car's top

SPECIFICATION

Engine: V12 cylinders with four overhead camshafts and four valves per cylinder

Capacity: 5935cc

Bore x stroke: 89x79.5mm

Maximum Power: 435bhp at 6000rpm

Maximum Torque: 556Nm at 5000rpm

Transmission: Five-speed automatic or six-speed manual

Suspension: Front: Independent, double wishbones and coil springs

Rear: Independent, lower wishbones with upper halfshaft links and coil springs

Length: 4692mm

Width: 1830mm

Height: 1243mm

Weight: 1800kg

Top Speed: 185mph

0-62mph: 5.0 seconds (manual transmission)

speed of 185mph.

The stylists at Aston Martin also added a pair of distinctive vents in the GT's bonnet. These fed air to the engine and also helped to reduce under-bonnet temperatures. There was also a new mesh front grille with a subtle 'GT' badge on it.

Also unique to the DB7 GT were 18-inch light-alloy wheels with five spokes that allowed a good view of the massive, grooved brake discs with their four-piston calipers. The wheels were shod with high-performance, low-profile Bridgestone tyres to provide optimum levels of performance and grip. Meanwhile, electronic traction control went even further in helping to keep the GT on the road, but without distracting from the fun of driving the car.

Despite the extra sportiness, the GT was no stripped out racecar. Inside, the passengers were treated to a full leather interior, electrically controlled and heated front seats, climate control, six-speaker Kenwood stereo system with CD autochanger, carbon fibre trim and much more.

By the time the GT arrived, the DB7 was a full 10 years old and beginning to show its age. It was, though, a great finale to a great car.

DB9
2003

THE DB7 WAS A GREAT SUCCESS BUT, by the start of the 21st century, it was beginning to show its age. The Vanquish had shown the way forward with its space-age construction and this was the inspiration behind the DB7's replacement, the DB9.

A quick note on names is in order here. The obvious badge for the new car would have been DB8, but it was thought that this would cause confusion with the new 'baby' Aston Martin, the V8 Vantage, so the new V12-engined car was named DB9.

The DB9's lines were quite obviously an evolution of what came before it, yet more aggressive than the DB7 with more than a hint of Vanquish in the mix.

Construction-wise, the DB9 was streets ahead of the conventional DB7. It had an immensely stiff, bonded aluminium frame onto which the body panels were attached, using high-tech adhesives. The bonnet, roof and rear wings were aluminium, while the front wings and bootlid were composite. The entire structure was 25 percent lighter than the DB7 bodyshell.

The DB9 was powered by essentially the same V12 engine as used in the DB7 Vantage, but it was fettled to increase the maximum power to 450bhp and the torque to 570Nm.

To ensure a 50:50 weight distribution, the front-mounted engine was linked to a rear-mounted gearbox. Two transmissions were offered; a conventional six-speed manual or a six-speed automatic. The latter was revolutionary in that it used a 'shift by wire' gearchange instead of the usual selector lever; a system of buttons were used to select Park, Reverse, Drive or Neutral. It also gave the option of Formula One-style manual shifts using paddle controls on the steering column.

The DB9 had a plush and well-appointed cabin in the best Aston Martin traditions. As well as the usual leather, there was also an abundance of aluminium which was most evident in the dash. The instruments had three-dimensional aluminium faces which were 'floodlit' rather than back-lit, to make them look extra-special at night. Unusually, the rev-counter ran anti-clockwise and did not have a conventional red line because the rev limit varied (depending on the engine's mileage, how recently the engine had been started and the ambient temperature). Instead, a red warning symbol came on when maximum revs were reached.

Wood is traditional on Aston Martins, but for the DB9 the designers steered clear of small amounts of 'glued on' veneer trim and opted instead for a large, solid, piece in the centre of the dash top and, optionally, in the door trims as well.

The DB9 was produced in coupe and open-top Volante styles.

SPECIFICATION

Engine: V12 cylinders with four overhead camshafts and four valves per cylinder

Capacity: 5935cc

Bore x stroke: 89x79.5mm

Maximum Power: 450bhp at 6000rpm

Maximum Torque: 570Nm at 5000rpm

Transmission: Six-speed manual or six-speed automatic

Suspension: Front: Independent, double wishbones and coil springs

Rear: Independent, double wishbones with longitudinal control arms and coil springs

Length: 4710mm

Width: 1875mm

Height: 1270mm

Weight: 1760kg

Top Speed: 186mph

0-60mph: 4.9 seconds

Vanquish S

2004

The updated car was an evolution of the original Vanquish and had the same revolutionary extruded aluminium and carbon fibre body structure, which was hand-assembled at Aston Martin's Newport Pagnell factory. It was, though, subtly updated. At the front, there was a more rounded radiator grille and a deeper front spoiler to aid the aerodynamics. At the back of the car, meanwhile, the bootlid was redesigned with a larger lip spoiler and an integral central brake light.

The 6.0-litre V12 engine also received attention. A new cylinder head design, revised mapping, new injectors and other changes increased the maximum power by no less than 60bhp to give 520bhp at

THE ORIGINAL VANQUISH WAS AN impressive machine, but Aston Martin made it even better with the S version, which was unveiled at the Paris Motor Show in 2004.

7000rpm, while peak torque was raised to 577Nm at 5800rpm.

The power went through the same six-speed manual transmission with paddle shifters, but the final drive ratio gearing was shortened to give better mid-range performance; for instance, the 50-70mph acceleration time (in top gear) was improved by almost two seconds.

SPECIFICATION

Engine: V12 cylinders with four overhead camshafts and four valves per cylinder

Capacity: 5935cc

Bore x stroke: 89x79.5mm

Maximum Power: 520bhp at 7000rpm

Maximum Torque: 5477Nm at 5800rpm

Transmission: Six-speed manual with Auto Shift Manual/Select Shift Manual (ASM/SSM) electro-hydraulic control system

Suspension: Front: Independent, double wishbones and coil springs

Rear: Independent, double wishbones with upper halfshaft links and coil springs

Length: 4665mm

Width: 1923mm

Height: 1238mm

Weight: 1875kg

Top Speed: 200+mph

0-62mph: 4.8 seconds

To cope with the extra power, the Vanquish S received revised brakes with larger discs and six-piston front calipers, while the suspension was lowered and treated to uprated springs and dampers. The steering, too, was changed to make its response 20 percent faster.

All this combined to ensure that the Vanquish S was an even faster and more exciting car to drive. Indeed, at the time of its launch, it was the fastest production car Aston Martin had ever built.

However, it was also a luxury car, as you'd expect of an Aston Martin. The interior remained essentially the same as the original Vanquish, but received some detail updates, and was a sumptuous place to be, with aluminium, leather, Wilton carpet and Alcantara in abundance. As before, buyers could choose between two seats with luggage space behind, or two small seats for children in the back.

Because the cars were hand-built to order, customers could specify whatever interior and exterior colours they wished, and you could even have stainless steel plates engraved with your name attached to the door sills.

V8 Vantage

2005

THE V8 VANTAGE WAS FIRST HINTED at in 2003, when Aston Martin showed the AMV8 Vantage concept car at the Detroit Motor Show. The reaction to the idea of a 'baby' Aston Martin was phenomenal and so the car went into production two years later as the V8 Vantage.

The name was, perhaps, a little confusing, because the Vantage badge was traditionally used for high-performance variants, whereas the V8 Vantage was an entry-level Aston Martin.

Not to worry, though, because it was still a superb car; smaller and more agile than its big brothers, the DB9 and Vanquish, yet with the traditional Aston

Martin attributes of style and quality, mixed with a good dose of high-tech.

Underneath the stunningly good-looking body lay a bonded aluminium frame (derived from that of the DB) onto which the aluminium, steel and composite panels were attached. The result was a light, stiff and strong structure.

The body was finished off with state-of-the-art lighting, with LED (light emitting diode) indicators, side repeaters, rear and brake lights. High-power xenon headlamps were an option.

As its name suggests, the V8 Vantage was powered by an all-new 4.3-litre V8 engine made entirely of aluminium and capable of producing a healthy 380bhp and 417Nm of torque. The engine was mounted well back under the bonnet to help give an even weight distribution to aid handling. This was helped by mounting the gearbox at the rear of the car and linking it to the engine with a carbon fibre propshaft. The gearbox itself was either a six-speed manual or a six-speed automatic with manual changes via Formula One-style paddle shifters.

Unlike the DB9, the V8 Vantage was strictly a two-seater car, while an opening rear hatch allowed a good amount of luggage to be carried, making it a practical long-distance tourer.

And the interior made it a car you'd be happy to be in for long periods. It combined traditional, hand-trimmed leather and aluminium with modern ergonomics and style, and high-tech options such as satellite navigation and a Bluetooth telephone link.

The V8 Vantage was followed by an open-top Roadster version.

SPECIFICATION

Engine: V8 cylinders with four overhead camshafts and four valves per cylinder

Capacity: 4300cc

Bore x stroke: 89x86mm

Maximum Power: 460bhp at 6500rpm

Maximum Torque: 542Nm at 5000rpm

Transmission: Six-speed manual or six-speed automatic with manual shifts

Suspension: Front: Independent, double wishbones and coil springs

Rear: Independent, double wishbones and coil springs

Length: 4380mm

Width: 1865mm

Height: 1255mm

Weight: 1630kg

Top Speed: 175mph

0-62mph: 5.0 seconds

Rapide Concept
2006

AT THE 2006 DETROIT MOTOR SHOW in the USA, Aston Martin unveiled an exciting concept car. And to everyone's surprise, it was a four-door, high-performance sports saloon, in much the same manner as the Lagonda of the 1970s.

The Rapide, as the car was called, was obviously based on the DB9 coupe, but was stretched to improve accommodation for rear passengers and to make room for the extra doors. Aston Martin was able to achieve this relatively simply by virtue of its VH (Vertical/Horizontal) architecture that formed the backbone of the DB9. The extruded aluminium construction could be modified in both length and width, providing a myriad of packaging options, and the bonded structure was mated with the aluminium and composite bodywork.

The result was an impressive machine that had real presence while, at the same time, being slick and elegant. The Rapide concept car had different headlamps to the DB9 – more angular projector items – and a novel transparent roof that could be made opaque at the touch of a button.

Inside, the dashboard was based on that of the DB9 but with a new centre console, dials based on Swiss watches, and different trim finishes. Rear passengers were treated to extra legroom, a DVD player and even access to the satellite navigation system because, said Aston Martin, it was vital that both driver and passengers should be involved in route planning. The front seats, meanwhile, could lie flat so you could catch forty winks during a long, cross-continental journey.

At the back of the car was a lifting rear hatch that gave access to the useful luggage area. On the show car, this was equipped with a chess board, pack of cards and a champagne chiller! On a more practical note, Aston Martin claimed that there was room for three sets of golf clubs, or up to four pairs of skis.

Up front, meanwhile, the Rapide was powered by the same V12 engine as the DB9, but uprated to 480bhp and mated to a Touchtronic automatic gearbox with fingertip manual control when required. To counter the power, the car was the first Aston Martin to be equipped with carbon brakes and calipers.

At the time the Rapide was shown, Aston Martin insisted it would remain a concept car. However, later in 2006, it was announced that a production version would follow by 2009.

SPECIFICATION

Engine: V12 cylinders with four overhead camshafts and four valves per cylinder
Capacity: 5935cc
Bore x stroke: 89x79.5mm
Maximum Power: 480bhp at 6000rpm
Maximum Torque: 570Nm at 5000rpm
Transmission: Six-speed automatic
Suspension: Front: Independent, double wishbones and coil springs
Rear: Independent, double wishbones with longitudinal control arms and coil springs
Length: 4980mm
Width: 1915mm
Height: 1358mm
Weight: 1920kg
Top Speed: 185mph (estimated)
0-62mph: 5.0 seconds (estimated)

DBS
2007

THE 2006 JAMES BOND FILM CASINO Royale featured a new Aston Martin – the DBS. At the time, the company gave very little away about the new car, although it was very obviously a tuned version of the DB9.

The car in the film featured a new front spoiler, sideskirts and rear valance,

that some of the bodywork would be carbon fibre to keep the weight down. The interior, too, appeared to be lightweight, with no rear seats and Alcantara and aluminium trim.

The DBS had the same V12 engine as the DB9 but tuned (possibly with superchargers) to produce in excess of 500bhp. Ceramic brakes were a possibility, too.

The DBS was due to go into production at the end of 2007.

SPECIFICATION

Engine: V12 cylinders with four overhead camshafts and four valves per cylinder

Capacity: 5935cc

Bore x stroke: 89x79.5mm

Maximum Power: 500bhp (estimated)

Maximum Torque: 600Nm (estimated)

Transmission: Six-speed manual

Suspension: Front: Independent, double wishbones and coil springs

Rear: Independent, double wishbones with longitudinal control arms and coil springs

Length: 4710mm (estimated)

Width: 1875mm (estimated)

Height: 1270mm (estimated)

Weight: n/a

Top Speed: 190mph (estimated)

0-62mph: 4.6 seconds (estimated)

and air vents in the bonnet, to give a more aggressive appearance than the DB9. Although few details were available at the time of writing, it is likely

James Bond
and Aston Martin

THINK ASTON MARTIN AND IT'S hard not to think of the 007 spy, James Bond. However, in the first Ian Fleming novel, Casino Royale, published in 1953, Bond actually drove a 1933 Bentley convertible with a 4.5-litre supercharged engine, not an Aston Martin. This was, according to the story, Bond's own personal car, which he'd owned since before the Second World War. This Bentley was then destroyed during a car chase in the next book, Moonraker, and replaced by a more modern 1953 Bentley Mark VI. Then, in

the novels Thunderball and On Her Majesty's Secret Service, Bond drove a Bentley Mark II Continental which, again, was supercharged, so it was obvious that the spy enjoyed fast British cars.

Bond first drove an Aston Martin in the novel Goldfinger, published in 1959. In this book, Fleming gave his hero a DB Mark III to drive (although he incorrectly called it a DBIII, which was actually a racing car) and described it as having front and rear lights that could change colour, reinforced bumpers, a Colt .45 pistol hidden in a compartment under the driver's seat, and a homing device.

However, by the time the film of the same name came along in 1964, the

DB5 was the current model and so this was the car used by the screen Bond, although the two silver ones supplied by Aston Martin for use in the film were, in fact, almost identical-looking DB4 Mark 5s.

The car driven by actor Sean Connery was 'modified' by Q Branch with a range of special options, including twin Browning machine guns hidden behind the front sidelights, oil slick dispenser, smoke screen, extendable front and rear overriders for ramming, extendable bulletproof steel barrier behind the rear window, revolving cutters in the wheel hubs, passenger ejector seat and revolving numberplates. A generation of schoolboys enjoyed playing with the detailed Corgi model of the car. The same DB5 was used again by Sean Connery in Thunderball in 1965.

The 1967 film On Her Majesty's Secret Service featured a metallic green Aston Martin DBS, driven by George Lazenby as James Bond. However, the car didn't appear much in the film and the only 'extra' shown was a hidden compartment in the glovebox for a sniper's rifle. The DBS also appeared very briefly in the background of a scene in the next film,

Diamonds Are Forever, when workers at Q Branch could be seen lowering missiles into its bonnet.

James Bond then flirted with Lotuses for a while before returning to Aston Martin for The Living Daylights in 1987. Timothy Dalton played Bond in that film and he drove a charcoal-grey

ABOVE The Vanquish, from the James Bond film Die Another Day, on display during the 2002 British International Motorshow

V8 Vantage Volante endowed with extendable side skis, retractable spikes in the tyres, missiles, lasers in the wheel hubs, signal-intercepting smart radio, head-up display and rocket propulsion. Later in the film it was 'winterised' with a hardtop and essentially became a coupe. The car could also be set to self-destruct.

Bond then drove BMWs in subsequent films, basically because the German company was willing to pay handsomely to have its products shown.

Early in the 1995 film Golden Eye, Bond, played by Pierce Brosnan (who, incidentally, owned a Vanquish in real life), was seen driving an Aston Martin DB5, the implication being that it was his own personal car. It was, though, equipped with a refrigerator in the centre armrest that held (of course) a bottle of champagne and two glasses, and there was a communication system that included a fax machine. The same car appeared again briefly in Tomorrow Never Dies in 1997.

Interestingly, for the next film, The World is Not Enough, Bond was filmed driving a DB5 to M16's Scottish headquarters but the scene was not used in the final cut. There was,

though, a brief 'thermal satellite' image at the end of the movie showing the Aston Martin in Istanbul.

The 2002 film Die Another Day featured an Aston Martin V12, which Q called the 'Vanish' on account of its adaptive camouflage that could make the car all but invisible at the touch of a button! This Aston Martin was driven by actor Pierce Brosnan and also featured a passenger ejector seat, front-firing rockets, bonnet-mounted target-seeking guns and spike-producing tyres.

In the 2006 film Casino Royale, James Bond was played by Daniel Craig. Early on in the story he won a now classic Aston Martin DB5 in a game of poker. Later, though, he drove a Q Branch-prepared Aston Martin DBS V12 – a car that wasn't even on sale to the public at the time. The only gadgets shown in the car were a secret compartment for a Walther P99 pistol and an emergency medical kit which Bond handily used to save his own life! The car later flipped over and crashed – a stunt that proved very difficult to execute on account of the car's low centre of gravity and excellent handling.

Over the years Aston Martin has become synonymous with James Bond and there is no doubt that the films have been of tremendous benefit in promoting the marque worldwide.

BELOW The two stars of Die Another Day - Aston Martin and Pierce Brosnan

E-TYPE JAGUAR

Series 1: 1961–1968

THE E-TYPE ROADSTER AND FIXED head coupé were unveiled at the Geneva Motor Show in March 1961 to universal acclaim in a world premiere. Two E-types were sent to Geneva with one example being presented to journalists in the Eaux Vives Park, while the other was the sensation of the year on the stand at the Geneva Show. It was also well received when it made its bow at the New York Motor Show the following month and America soon fell in love with the marque. Its futuristic styling and outstanding technical attributes convinced not only the motoring journalists, but also made a deep impression on the public.

The cars featured a monocoque – French for "single" (mono) and "shell" (coque) – body with a front sub-frame, two seats and a rear luggage door on the coupé. The first automotive application of the monocoque technique was Lancia's 1923 Lambda and a few years later in 1934, both Chrysler and Citroën built the first mass-produced monocoque vehicles with the innovative Chrysler Airflow and the Traction Avant respectively. So while the monocoque technology was not a totally new innovation, improvements in the manufacturing process now allowed separate parts to be combined into single stampings that reduced weight and assembly costs, as well as increasing structural rigidity and improving door fitment.

Costing £2,097 for the roadster and £2,196 for the coupé (a revelation when Aston Martin's rival DB4 retailed at £3,968), the E-types were initially sold with a three-carburettor version of the 3,781cc six-cylinder XK engine that produced 265 bhp at 5,500 rpm and was meshed to a four-speed Moss gearbox.

Although the engine was already 13 years old, it was defined by many as the most advanced production engine in the world and having powered the XK series since 1948, it would continue to be installed in Jaguars until 1986. The original 3,442cc engine had been developed during the Second World War specifically to drive a new luxury saloon (that would emerge in 1950 as the Mark VII) at speeds of 100 mph.

Featuring a double overhead camshaft, a cast-iron block and a seven-bearing crank with an aluminium cylinder head, it also boasted separate timing chains (top and bottom) and the two

LEFT A 1962 E-type with an eye catching design

RIGHT Headturning
wire wheels

valves per cylinder optimised perform-ance giving 160 bhp at 5,000 rpm. Refinements carried out during the 1950s increased the capacity of the engine bringing the power to 220 bhp from the enlarged 3,781cc that drove the Mark IX saloon and XK150 and culmi-nated in the power plant that was unveiled in the first E-types that were able to do 0-60 in 6.9 seconds.

Other modifications included the fit-ting of a manual choke and a separate header tank between the radiator and the engine that reduced the necessary height and allowed for the design of the sleek body that has been admired for almost 50 years. Obviously there were other measures that individual owners could take to increase the engine's power such as replacing the SU carbs with Webers although the North American federal exhaust emission reg-ulations meant that cars headed for that continent from 1968 were supplied with two Zenith-Stromberg carburet-tors which, combined with a revised manifold, produced less residue at low speeds.

Early problems, however, included drastic oil consumption (sometimes as much as 200-300 miles per pint) and a tendency to overheat but many enthusi-asts still yearn for one of the first cars off the production line. It wasn't until a sec-ond fan was installed on the Series 2 cars in 1968 that the latter problem was overcome. But, such was the reliability of the engine that it was claimed owners could expect it to last for up to 200,000 miles if properly looked after.

A bigger bore offered a larger 4,236cc engine in 1964 but the arrangement of four of the six cylinders had to be moved slightly in order to keep the overall block size the same. Other mod-ifications included straightening the inlet manifold tracts, installing a Lucas alternator instead of the original dynamo and a pre-engaged starter motor - all of which gave the larger engine the same power output as the 3.8 litre version but with increased torque (up from 260lb/ft to 283lb/ft at 4,000 rpm). It also discouraged prolonged cruising over 5,000 rpm which could on occasion result in crankshaft damage and a hefty repair bill. The on the road price for these cars was £1,896 for the roadster while the coupé retailed at £1,992.

The gearbox had also been around for some time, in this case since 1946 and

would be utilised in every manual Jaguar until 1964. With the same ratios as had been used on the XK150S, the four-speed box was married to a 10" Borg and Beck single plate clutch but it became synonymous with a crashing first gear and changing between the other gears was only made easier by mastering the art of double declutching. This problem was alleviated by the introduction of a new all-synchromesh gearbox that coincided with the arrival of the 4.2 litre engine in 1964. Now lubricated, inertia baulk rings ensured

the 2-plus-2 that was unleashed in March 1966. This conventional box offered three selections – L (Lock-up), D1 and D2. With the central T handle positioned in D1, the car automatically changed through all the gears but if you selected D2 only second and top were available which provided a smoother ride and greater fuel economy. The new model was 9" longer than the coupé and boasted a revised rear bulkhead that allowed the addition of a rear seat.

The front suspension had been taken from the design that had worked so well over the years with the D-type, with forged wishbones being used top and bottom along with a torsion bar and telescopic dampers. But it was the set-up at the rear of the car that raised a few eyebrows.

Independent suspension had been tried on various cars built in Europe but without much success. Jaguar, however, had mastered the problems where others had failed and the layout designed under the supervision of William Heynes caused great interest when unveiled. Rather than having the body mounted on leaf springs that keep each opposing wheel perpendicular to the other, Heynes' team created a steel sub-

LEFT The Jaguar 4.2 litre E-type 2-plus-2 from 1966

that the gears could not be engaged until they were synchronised which, together with a Laycock diaphragm clutch, provided a smoother ride.

Customers were first given the option of an automatic gearbox (at an extra cost of £140) with the introduction of

frame that housed the entire suspension as well as the differential, hub carriers and disc brakes. With this assembly connected to the body by just four rubber mountings (plus two radius arms and their respective mountings), this innovative design allowed each wheel to independently rise and fall vertically along the surface of the road thereby improving the handling and safety of the car while providing a smoother ride for its passengers. While this was of great comfort while driving, it was a hindrance to maintenance and even the simplest of tasks often involved dropping the whole unit out of the back end of the car.

The E-type was steered via a rack and pinion system that was popular at the time. With the rack running across the car behind the radiator joining the two front wheels, the driver's instructions were transmitted from the steering wheel via a universally-jointed steering column. With the ability to turn the steering wheel two and a half rotations to change from one lock to the other, it gave the E-type a turning circle of around 35 feet - not bad when you consider today's XF at 16' 3" long (compared to the E-type at 14' 7") has a

turning circle of 37 feet.

One of the few areas to come under frequent criticism was the brakes but Jaguar, always alert to negative comments and the publicity that accompanied them, were constantly redeveloping their set-up in an attempt to provide a braking system that adequately matched the performance needs of the E-type. January 1962 saw the introduction of modified master cylinders while a revised pedal and power leaver followed four months later. Just over a year later, thicker rear discs and better callipers further alleviated the stopping problems although the braking system that accompanied the arrival of the 4.2 car was altogether better and provided fewer heart-stopping moments.

The E-types were supplied with wire wheels, something that has gone out of fashion today with the technological advances in their alloy counterparts but it is a throwback to a more romantic era of motoring that many find aesthetically pleasing. Originally fitted with Dunlop RS 6.40x15 crossplies, by late 1965 it was Dunlop's SP41 radials that the car would be wearing - although it was possible to order racing tyres for a

ABOVE Series 1 E-type Jaguar on display

car to enhance performance. The advantage of the radial tyre was that its construction allowed for the sidewalls and crown of the tyre to have separate functions which gave greater traction and a longer lifespan.

As previously mentioned, it is easy to see that the E-type's distinctive looks were largely inherited from the D-type. Malcolm Sayer was credited with the end result although Sir William Lyons was also responsible for artistic input. The front end of the car was a framework of tubing that was designed to take the stresses of carrying the engine and front suspension. This was anchored to

the monocoque shell that ran backwards from the front bulkhead, encompassing in the passenger compartment and the rear of the car. The curved panels were constructed by Abbey Panels while Pressed Steel Fisher built the inner sections with the whole lot being put together at Browns Lane.

As with many roadsters, it was the two hollow sills along each side of this section (between the wheel arches) that provided the greatest strength of the construction. The structure was further strengthened by the steel floorwells (that were revised at the end of 1961 as taller customers complained about the

lack of leg room), the transmission housing and propshaft tunnel as well as a transverse member running under the seats. Box members were welded to the floor of the boot and the inner wheel arches with others added to the rear bulkhead (which was also modified to allow for the seat to be adjusted) to take the strain of the rear suspension radius arms. Obviously, the roof of the coupé provided added strength and the roadster later came with an option to buy a glassfibre hard-top (at a cost of £76) that could conveniently be fitted with the mohair hood in place. As a soft-top, the roadster was reasonably comfortable and waterproof with the hood up, however, it was prone to excessive wind noise despite the fact that each hood was tailored to the individual car in Jaguar's own trim shop.

The bonnet was constructed in three sections (centre and wings with the joints concealed by chromium plated moulding) and was designed to be hinged at the front end of the car, thereby allowing easy access to the engine compartment as required. The bonnet might seem heavy to lift, but that action was aided by counterbalanced springs and the external Budget

locks were replaced with internal versions in September 1961 to cure vibration issues. The "muscle car look" was further enhanced by the power bulge and accompanying louvres (that also helped with cooling the engine) as well as the distinctive front lights. These may have looked attractive but the toughened glass covers dispersed the light beams and failed to provide adequate lighting when driving at night in adverse weather conditions - a problem rectified with the introduction of the 4.2 model that boasted more powerful sealed beam headlamps. At the other end of the car was the luggage area, very restricted on the roadster – although there was an area behind the seats where smaller items could be stowed.

The rear lights differed on the roadster and the coupé due to obvious restrictions of the body while the car was finished off with decorative chrome trim and a bar that bisected the oval air intake. A trio of two-speed wipers were installed to keep the large wrap-around windscreen clear and this only added to the individuality of the E-type.

The interior of the cockpit was just as eye-catching as the car itself, with a central aluminium panel housing many of

LEFT Series 1 E-type Jaguar from the front

the instruments as well as leaving space for a radio and twin speakers. White figures on black faces adorned the Smiths oil pressure, water temperature, fuel and ammeter gauges while the matching speedometer (calibrated to 160 mph) and rev counter that incorporated a clock were traditionally positioned in front of the driver. There was a separate key ignition switch and a starter button.

The aluminium finish was repeated on the handbrake shroud while the Coventry Timber Bending Company produced the steering wheel which was finished in wood with three aluminium spokes. Connolly hide adorned the bucket seats above a plush carpet (again, these seats would be improved in the 4.2 along with many other interior modifications) with seat-belt anchoring points standard since January 1962. The coupé saw the introduction of an optional heated rear screen in April 1962.

Jaguar, noting that families wanted to be seen in their flagship vehicle and having to keep up with competitors who had already introduced rear seats for children in their sports cars, introduced a 2-plus-2 in March 1966 that was 9" longer than the standard coupé and incorporated a small bench seat in the rear. To accomplish this, Jaguar had increased the size of the cockpit – in height as well as length that gave the car a more upright appearance – and the doors were now more than 8" wider. There was more room for luggage, a parcel shelf and a bigger transmission tunnel that could accommodate an automatic gearbox while the springs and dampers were uprated to deal with the extra weight.

Jaguar made minor refinements to the E-type Series 1 at the end of the following year – including exposing the headlights to improve visibility – and these cars have affectionately become known as the Series 1 ½ as they bore many of the modifications that were featured in the fully revamped Series 2 that Jaguar unveiled in October 1968. The previous eared hub-caps were replaced by circular ones and a mirror was added to the driver's door.

Inside the cockpit there were more modifications including a revamped facia with rocker switches being replaced and a hazard warning light being added. The heater controls were also revised along with the demisting vents to provide better operation. One main feature of this car was the new

ABOVE Series 1 E-type Jaguar from the rear

doors which had had to be redesigned to incorporate "burst proof" locks as dictated by American legislation.

The Series 1 had outdone Jaguar's initial expectations and it had taken time to get production up to a level that could come anywhere near coping with the demand. More than 2,000 cars were sold by the end of 1961 (and hasty production measures had to be put in place to cope), a figure that was double the company's original estimate for total sales. Indeed, it had initially been envisaged that they might only sell 250 E-types, although this was quickly revised and overtaken. By the end of 1963, 12,491 cars had been built making it the best-selling Jaguar sports car ever - a figure that smashed the previous record of 12,055 held by the XK120 which had taken five years! 1966 was also to prove a record year with 6,880 cars being built - the most popular being the 2-plus-2 at 2,627.

177225·TN

E-type Jaguar
Series 2: 1968–1971

RIGHT A 1970 E-type Jaguar

WHEN THE SERIES 2 WAS OFF-icially unveiled at the 1968 London Motor Show, many of the obvious modifications that had shown up earlier on the Series 1 ½ were more apparent. Yes, the headlights were bigger and now external (as opposed to being covered) and thereby reduced the car's top speed by a couple of miles per hour but the air intake had been enlarged by 68 per cent which improved the airflow. This was due in part to compensate for the overheating problems that had dogged the Series 1 but it was also dictated by the new air conditioning system that was to be offered as an optional extra on cars exported to the US. Other optional extras included power steering and chromium-plated disc wheels instead of the traditional wire counterparts. One other modification that alleviated

the overheating was the replacing of the single engine-driven fan with a twin electric-fan unit to cool the new crossflow radiator.

One of the main differences between the two models was that Jaguar dispensed with the 3.8 version and only offered the Series 2 with the larger 4.2 engine. The cars retailed at £2,163 for the roadster, £2,273 for the coupé and £2,668 for the 2-plus-2 making any of the three models a reasonably priced alternative to many of Jaguar's competitors of the era.

The braking system received its first major overhaul in seven years as the original Lockheed units were ditched in favour of Girling brakes with three cylinder callipers. This increased the area of the discs used for braking and provided increased stopping power.

Externally, the original thin

bumpers were replaced with larger wrap-around ones and the decorative intake bar became thicker. The rear lights were also enlarged and mounted beneath, rather than above the bumper while twin reversing lights were introduced. The exhaust tail pipes now protruded from either side of the car due to the number plate being lowered.

Structurally, little had changed from the Series 1. The rake of the front windscreen on the 2-plus-2 was increased from 46 ½ degrees to 53 ½ degrees, thereby moving the bottom of the screen towards the front of the car to make it appear less upright. This did, however, mean that there was not enough room for the three-wiper set-up and the car reverted to the more traditional pair of wipers.

In the cockpit, right-hand drive cars benefited from the US-style interior that saw a new dashboard installed. The final month of 1968 saw the fitting of a steering column lock while the following May saw the introduction of perforated leather trim and modified head restraints. Jaguar continued to tinker with numerous areas of the car including redesigned

camshafts in November 1969, a revised clutch operating rod in March 1970 and a revised handbrake lever on the 2-plus-2 two months later.

The first full year of production, 1969, saw a record 9,948 cars built at Browns Lane. This total comprised 4,287 roadsters, 2,397 coupés and 3,264 2-plus-2s but numbers dive-bombed over the next two years with only 3,781 being delivered in 1971. It was time for a change and Jaguar responded with the Series 3.

E-type Jaguar
Series 3: 1971–1975

MUCH HAS BEEN WRITTEN IN THE intervening years about the disappointment felt by many E-type enthusiasts when the Series 3 was introduced in March 1971. True, the car did have a larger and more powerful 5.3 litre V12 engine but it was widely argued that the car into which it was installed was outdated and outclassed. Ironically though, the 14,983 V12s that were built have today become one of the most sought-after versions of the E-type.

The launch took place at Palm Beach and was attended by Sir William Lyons on what was his farewell trip to the US. At the age of 69, he was retiring the following year. He was accompanied by Harry Mundy, one of the brains behind the V12 engine that Jaguar hoped would keep them competitive in America. Jaguar initially offered the Series 3 with an option of the 4.2 XK engine or the new V12 but soon withdrew the former as demand for the 5.3 grew.

The 5.3 was the only V12 of the era that was manufactured in significant numbers; both Ferrari and Lamborghini had their own versions of the V12 but these were produced in relatively small quantities. In order to cope with the new power plants, Jaguar spent £3 million upgrading its Radford factory so that it could cope with the manufacture of these larger units.

As with the original 3.8 engine, the 5.3 was not specifically designed for the E-type. It had begun its life during the 1950s with racing in mind, although it was temporarily shelved once Jaguar pulled out of competing in 1956 and did not enjoy a test run until August 1964. It had been envisaged to run the engine in the 1965 Le

Mans race but Jaguar did not have a suitable car.

Work began on a mid-engined racer, similar in set-up to the Formula One cars of the time and work began on the XJ13. The new prototype was not entered at the following year's Le Mans and – when Jaguar merged with the British Motor Corporation – testing suggested that it wasn't as fast as anticipated. The company was particularly worried about news of the project being leaked to the press as rumours of a V12 E-type would have dramatically hit sales of the six-cylinder model and Jaguar simply weren't ready to put the new engine into production. It was a case of back to the drawing board.

So it was that 1971 saw the revamped V12 engine being "roadtested" in the Series 3 in preparation for its installation in the new XJ12 that arrived the following year. Jaguar used the E-type as a guinea pig so that any teething problems could be ironed out before the launch of its flagship saloon. The original intention had been to use a fuel injection system being developed by Brico but it was decided to stick with the traditional carburettor set-up and each set of three cylinders was fed by a

LEFT An American Series 3 E-type

RIGHT Series 3 E-type
Coupé

Zenith-Stromberg 175CDSE carb.

The Series 3 was only offered as a roadster and a 2-plus-2 coupé, both sharing the latter's longer wheelbase. This meant that the roadster gained extra luggage space as well as more room for seat adjustment. Obvious modifications included flared wheel arches and a bigger front air intake that housed a grill that was likened to a bird cage. An air scoop was also added underneath the intake to increase ventilation throughout the car. This was supplemented by an extractor grille on the luggage door of the 2-plus-2 and the rear pillars of roadsters that were fitted with hard-tops.

Changes to the suspension saw the use of longer wishbones from the Mark X/420G and driveshafts which increased the rear track of the Series 3 which now came with 6" steel wheels as standard rather than the wired predecessors. As the car was heavier than the Series 2, the braking system was overhauled as well, with ventilated Girling discs installed on the front and power steering was now standard. The rack and pinion was modified in December 1972 following a report of a car not heading in the direction dictated by the driver.

Roadster customers were given the option of going with the traditional four-speed manual or they could upgrade to the automatic gearbox that had been available on the 2-plus-2 for the previous five years. Until March 1973 the exhaust system ended in a four-pipe fantail but this, like the rest of the car, was prone to rust and was replaced by a twin outlet with a modified silencer.

Inside the cockpit, Jaguar attempted to modernise the E-type with a smaller, leather-trimmed steering wheel, perforated leather seats and a fresh air ventilation system. The 2-plus-2 saw the front seats raised to provide better visibility while also giving the rear passengers more foot room and it was now possible for those in the back to recline the seat in front of them to make exiting the car easier.

Prices had increased with the roadster retailing at a cost of £3,123 and the 2-plus-2 for £3,369 – still drastically less than their competitors – but Jaguar found that cars were sitting longer on the forecourts of dealerships and new customers were no longer having to join a waiting list. American legislation was also dictating modifications to the fuel

tank and that a roll bar must be added to the 2-plus-2. Other, global, factors were also thrown into the mix such as the Arab-Israeli war that had broken out in October 1973 causing oil prices to spiral out of control leading to a decrease in demand for fuel-thirsty cars.

It was therefore decided to cease pro-

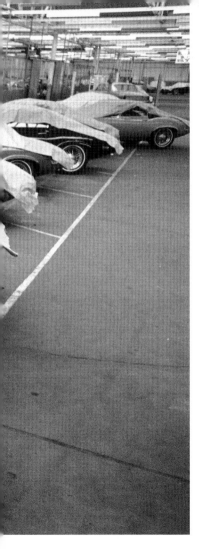

duction, with the final E-type being manufactured in September 1974; the decision was made public five months later. In a marketing ploy that backfired, Jaguar shipped all bar one of the final 50 roadsters in black, fitted them with wire wheels and installed a plaque in the dashboard of each that was signed by Sir William Lyons. (The penultimate car was painted in British Racing Green.) Sadly, these didn't fly out of the door as quickly as had been intended and several were sold at a reduced price. One of the reasons that these cars took so long to sell was that the public were reportedly keenly awaiting the arrival of the E-type's replacement, widely anticipated to be another sports car. As it turned out, the next Jaguar was the XJ-S which, at £8,900 (more than double the price of an E-type), was the most expensive vehicle the company had ever retailed.

Today, these V12 E-types are cherished as much for their refined ride as their look and suit those more interested in a luxury sports car rather than a rugged muscle car that provides a more lean driving experience. In 1975, however, it was the end of a golden era for British motoring as well as Jaguar themselves.

LEFT A line of new Jaguar E-type cars under dust sheets at Coventry, 1972

The pictures in this book were provided courtesy of the following:

GLYN-COCH CRAFT CENTRE www.glyn-coch.com

MICHAEL BAILIE – PHOTOGRAPHER www.michaelbailie.com

BY KIND PERMISSION OF OCTANE MAGAZINE www.octane-magazine.com

TIM COTTINGHAM www.astonmartin.com

KEITH ADAMS Motoring Writer

NEIL BRUCE www.brucephoto.co.uk

JON STROUD

SHUTTERSTOCK IMAGES www.shutterstock.com

© BRITISH MOTOR INDUSTRY HERITAGE TRUST

GETTY IMAGES
101 Bayham Street, London NW1 0AG

With special thanks to:
MG Car Club
Motor Industry Heritage Centre, Gaydon
John Pulford – Curator of Collections & Motoring, Brooklands Museum
Mark Hamilton – H&H Classic Auctions
Trevor Williams – Cowley Local History Society

Design & Artwork by: Alex Young

Published by: Demand Media Limited & G2 Entertainment Limited

Publishers: Jason Fenwick & Jules Gammond

Written by: Jon Stroud